RHYTHM GUITAR

By Harvey Vinson.

&

Amsco Publications
London/New York/Sydney

PHOTOGRAPHS:

by David Gahr
       8/Muddy Waters
       11/Chambers Brothers
       17/Harmonica Slim
       30/Bob Dylan
       36/The Butterfield Blues Band
       46/Bob Dylan
       55/B.B. King
       75/Donovan
       87/unknown
       100/Frank Zappa
       125/Dylan and Donovan

by Elliot Landy
       34/Ritchie Havens
       61/Jim Morrison
       64/John Lennon
       95Buddy Guy and Junior Wells
       101/Paul McCartney
       107/The Band
       113/Country Joe MacDonald
       115/Jimi Hendrix
       118/The Jimi Hendrix Experience

Courtesy of ATCO Records
       79/Cream

by Diana Davies
       51/Janis Joplin

by Jean Hammons
       24

Copyright © 1969 by Consolidated Music Publishers,
A Division of Music Sales Corporation, New York, NY.

Order No. AM 10687
US International Standard Book Number: 0.8256.4057.1
UK International Standard Book Number: 0.86001.924.1
Library of Congress Catalog Card Number: 76-84931

Exclusive Distributors:
Music Sales Corporation
257 Park Avenue South, New York, NY 10010 USA
Music Sales Limited
8/9 Frith Street, London W1V 5TZ England
Music Sales Pty. Limited
0 Rothschild Street, Rosebery, Sydney, NSW 2018, Australia

the United States of America by
raph and Printing Corporation

CONTENTS

PART I, INTRODUCTION TO RHYTHM GUITAR, 4
  Begin Here, 4
  More Stuff, 9
    Blues in A, 12
  Tuning Up, 13
  More Blues, 15
    Blues in D, 16
    Blues in D, 18
    Blues in G, 19
  7th Chords, 20
    Blues in A, 21
    Blues in G, 23

PART II, THE RHYTHM GUITARIST, 24
  Bar Chords, 24
    Blues in C, 25
    Blues in F, 27
  Special Effects, 28
    Blues in G, 29
    Blues in F, 31
    Blues in G, 32
  More Bar Chords, 33
    Blues in F, 34
    Progression, 36
  Skull Practice, 37
    Blues in G, 37
    Standard Progression, 38
    Standard Progression, 39
    Blues in C, 39
  Bar 7th Chords, 40
    Exercise, 41
    Exercise, 42
    Exercise, 43
    Progression in G, 44
    Blues in A, 45
  New Progressions, 47
    Rock Progression #1, 47
    Rock Progression #2, 48
    Rock Progression #3, 49
    Rock Progression #4, 50
  Minor Chords, 52
    Turn Around in C, 53
    Turn Around in G, 54
    Turn Around in F, 56
    Turn Around in C, 57
  New Bar Chords, 58
    Turn Around in Bb, 59
    Turn Around in D, 62

PART III, ADVANCED RHYTHM GUITAR
PLAYING, 63
  6th Chords, 63
    Blues in F, 66
    Blues in A, 67
    Blues in G, 69
  Arpeggios, 70
    Turn Around in C, 71
    Turn Around in D, 72
    Turn Around in A, 73

Connecting Chords, 74
    Guitar Boogie, 74
    Turn Around in C, 76
    Turn Around in G, 77
    Turn Around in A, 78
  Some New Things, 79
    Blues in Bb, 79
    Blues in G, 81
  Minor 6th and Minor 7th Chords, 83
    New Rock Progression, 85
  9th Chords, 86
    Jazz Blues in Bb, 88
    Turn Around in Bb, 89
    Blues in A, 90
  Rhythm Exercises, 91
    Exercise, 91
  New Chords, 95
    Rock Progression, 97
    Turn Around in A, 98
  The English Sound, 101
    New Progression, 102
    New Progression #2, 104
  Folk Rock, 105
    A Folk Style, 105
    Blues in G, 106
    Song, 108
    A Folk Progression, 110
  Advanced Rhythms, 111
    Blues in G, 112
    Blues in A, 114
    Blues in G, 116
  The Slide Chord, 117
    Blues in A, 119
    New Progression, 121
    Last Progression, 121
  Finishing Touches, 122
    Progression, 123
    Chord Chart, 124
    Progression, 124

APPENDIX A (Discography), 126
  Modern American, 126
  Folk Rock, 126
  Traditional Rhythm and Blues, 126
  The Detroit Soul Sound, 126
  Blues Bands, 126
  Modern English, 126

APPENDIX B (Suggestions for Buying a Guitar), 127
  Amplifiers, 127

APPENDIX C (Chord Diagrams), 128
  Open Chords, 128
  Movable Chords, 128

PART I
INTRODUCTION TO RHYTHM GUITAR

Begin Here

The most important thing to remember about rock 'n roll is that it's dance music. When you play rock, people dance; and dancing requires a strong, steady rhythm. That's where you come in.

As the rhythm guitarist in a rock band, it is your responsibility to keep the rhythm solid and moving. More than any other member, the rhythm guitarist can make or break a group.

We'll get to playing as soon as you pick up on a few fundamentals of technique and notation.

The only other piece of equipment you need is a guitar pick (also called a plectrum or flat-pick). They are generally made of a semi-flexible material and come in about three hundred different shapes and sizes. I generally recommend a large triangular pick for beginners; but if you come across a different size that feels right to you, by all means use it.

The pick is held between the index finger and the thumb of the right hand.

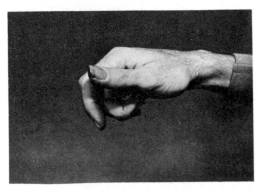

If you'll extend the index finger of your right hand,

If you're without an electric guitar or an amplifier, financial and other helpful hints on what and how to buy are on Page 136, Appendix C.

place the pick so that its point is about a quarter of an inch beyond the finger-tip,

then bring the thumb against the index finger, you'll be holding the pick correctly.

Although all performing is done in a standing position, most guitarists practice sitting down.

Cross your legs and rest the rounded indentation of the guitar on your right thigh. We'll worry about the left hand in a minute. With your right arm over the wide part of the guitar, poise your right hand above the strings at the waist of the guitar.

Let's start on your first strum. "Hold on!" you say, "My guitar is not in tune." For the time being, don't worry about tuning your guitar. Get a friend to tune it, or bring it to the music store where you bought your guitar and ask them to tune it for you. If neither friend nor music store is available, get a guitar pitch-pipe and tune your guitar to that. Later on, we'll get into tuning the guitar in detail.

Place the pick against the string nearest you. Don't play it yet. The only point of contact the right hand has with the guitar is with the pick. The string you've got your pick on is the 6th string and is also the thickest string.

Play the 6th string by pushing down and off the string with the pick coming to rest on the next string, the 5th string.

Play the 5th string the same way coming to rest on the 4th string. Play the 4th, the 3rd and the 2nd strings in the same manner finally playing the 1st string (the thinnest and the one nearest the floor). Now start over with the 6th string and repeat the whole process many times gradually speeding up until you're playing all six strings with one continuous downward motion.

Now we'll move to the left hand. The numbers 1 through 4 are used to indicate which left hand finger you should use. These numbers appear in circles in the chord diagrams in this book.

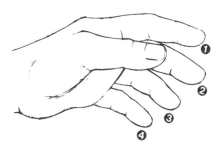

Here is your first chord, E Major.

E chord

Finger the E chord (courage now) and boldly strum it. Strum the chord again but this time place the pick on the 6th string and slowly glide over the strings, hitting them one by one. Listen to the sound produced by each string and try to get the idea of this chord in your ears as well as in your fingers. If any of the strings buzz or sound weak, check the left hand fingering. Make sure you're pushing down with the ends of your fingertips close to the frets. Fingernails obviously have to go.

After you've played the E chord for awhile and you're pretty sure you know it, try this next chord so we can get on to our first song.

A chord

Finger and play this A chord just like you did the E chord. Try to correct any buzzing strings before you go on.

Now start playing the A chord in a slow but steady rhythm using light, brisk down-strokes of the pick. As you're playing the A chord, think about the fingering of the E chord and try switching chords without losing the rhythm. Work on this for a bit but remember to keep the rhythm steady and *slow*. Using the same slow rhythm, start counting from 1 to 4 over and over as you're playing the chords. Now change chords each time you come to the "1" count. For example:

```
Play:    A . . . A . . . A . . . A . . . E . . . E . . . E . . . E . . A . . A . . A . . A
Count:   1 . . . 2 . . . 3 . . . 4 . . . 1 . . 2 . . . 3 . . . 4 . . 1 . . 2 . . . 3 . . . 4
```

What you've just done is set up a four beat (or count) rhythm. This is the rhythm of rock 'n roll. The two chords as we've been using them will fit to a number of songs, one of which is the very familiar *Skip To My Lou*.

This is a dance tune used for square dancing rather than rock 'n roll, but a dance tune none-the-less. Remember to keep the counts (or beats) smooth with no pauses when you change chords. Don't dig into the strings with the pick when you strum but use light and quick down-strokes. Practice this song until you can play it at the brisk speed typical of square dances. Sing along as you play.

SKIP TO MY LOU

	Lou,	Lou,	Skip to my Lou,		Lou,	Lou,	Skip to my Lou,	
Play:	A	A	A	A	E	E	E	E
Count:	1 . . . . . 2 . . . . 3 . . . . 4 . . . . . 1 . . . . . 2 . . . . . 3 . . . . 4 . . . . .

	Lou,	Lou,	Skip to my Lou,		Skip to my Lou, my dar. . . . . ling.			
Play:	A	A	A	A	E	E	A	A
Count:	1 . . . . . 2 . . . . 3 . . . . 4 . . . . . 1 . . . . . 2 . . . . . 3 . . . . . . 4 . . . . .

Having mastered this folk song, you now have the total concept of rhythm guitar: you kept the song moving with a steady, constant rhythm. Most rock songs are rhythmically no more complicated than this.

Here's an important point: every chord presented to you in this book is common knowledge among rock guitarists. You cannot afford to pass over any chord lightly, so don't go on until you are sure the A and E chords are firmly in your fingers.

More Stuff

Now for some more fundamentals of music notation.

Rhythm guitar parts are often written in what's known as a chord chart. By using a chord chart, the performer (that's you) can easily spot chord and rhythm changes. In the recording studios of the major record labels, one of the first things that musicians do is to make chord charts of the songs to be recorded. So, from now on, chord charts will be used to illustrate the chords and rhythms most commonly used in rock tunes.

All music is written on a standard music staff of five lines:

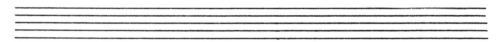

Don't get excited. You don't have to read music to get meaning out of the music staff. The vertical lines on the staff are called *bar lines*. The space between the bar lines is called a *measure*. (When somebody says to play the first three bars of a tune, they mean the first three measures.)

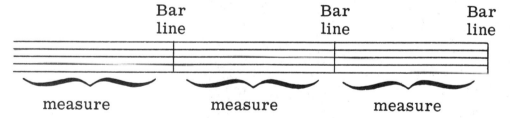

So far so good. The Trebel Clef Sign is found at the beginning of each line of music.

The $\mathbf{C}$ at the beginning of the staff is an abbreviation for Common Time meaning four beats (or counts) to each measure.

Count: 1   2   3   4

Wedge-marks ⟋⟋⟋⟋ on the staff indicate when a chord is to be sounded. Strum the chord once for each wedge-mark. In this example, strum the A chord once for each beat.

Count: 1   2   3   4

Using the music staff, here is a chord chart for *Skip To My Lou*. Compare this method of notating chords and rhythm with the method used in Lesson One.

Count: 1   2   3   4   1   2   3   4   1   2   3   4   1   2   3   4

A new chord to learn: D Major.

D chord

Notice that in the chord diagram, the 6th string is indicated by a line of dashes. When a string is shown this way, it means that you do not strum that string when you strum the chord. In this case, strum only the first five strings and *not* the 6th string.

Play the following two exercises to help familiarize yourself with this new chord.

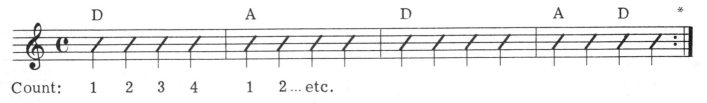

Count: 1   2   3   4   1   2...etc.

Count: 1   2   3   4...etc.

* ⟋⟋ is a repeat sign. It means to go back to the beginning and play the music again.

You'll have a much easier time playing these two chords together if you'll leave the 3rd finger of the left hand in contact with the string when you make the chord changes. After you play the A chord, pick up the 1st and 2nd fingers and slide the 3rd finger up (towards you) one fret. This puts the 3rd finger in position for the D chord. As a rule, try never to lose contact with the fingerboard when changing chords unless it can't be helped.

After you're sure you understand chord charts, and you can play the new chord (D), we'll get to work on a progression of chords derived from the blues.

The so called "blues progression" is *the* most important progression of chords in rock 'n roll. Songs like Elvis Presley's "Hounddog" and Chuck Berry's "Memphis" of the mid-50's to songs like "Mustang Sally" and the Beatles' "Flying" in the late 60's all are based on the same progression of chords: the blues progression.* Let's play one.

Play the following blues progression in A a few times starting on the slow side and gradually speeding up each time. You can tap your foot if you want to rather than counting to keep the beat.

Blues in A

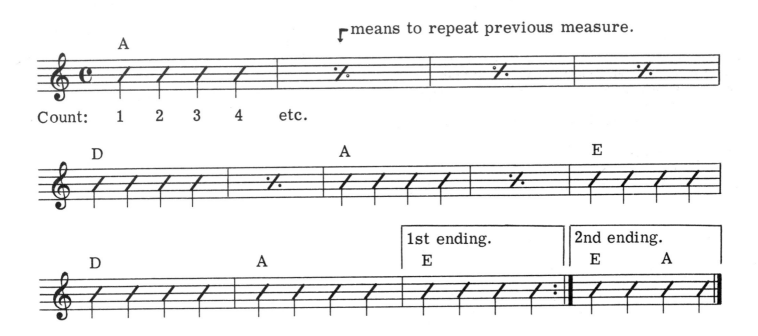

The second time through, the 2nd ending is used instead of the 1st ending. As there is no repeat sign at the end of the 2nd ending, the piece ends there.

If you'll count the number of measures from the beginning to the end of the 1st ending, you'll find that the blues is 12 measures (or bars) long. Playing through the repeat with the 2nd ending, the length is 12 times two. 12 bar blues is the most widely used of the many blues forms. It is referred to as "12 bar blues" no matter how many repeats you take.

Don't be afraid to play this blues progression 36 times, or so. Get the feeling of it inside you—it is that important. Try playing it at a few different speeds until the progression begins to feel "right" to you.

If it just doesn't sound good to you, maybe you better go to the next lesson now and come back to this.

*Come to think of it, John Lee Hooker, a beautiful country blues singer and guitarist, once said, "When you get right down to where it's at, everything comes from the blues."

Tuning Up

Every musician, sooner or later, has to come to grips with the problem of tuning his instrument. When you're playing along and something just doesn't sound right, you can almost bet that your guitar is out of tune. The more you play with a tuned guitar, the easier you can tell when it is out of tune. The person who suffers the most from an out-of-tune instrument is you and your ears. So keep your ax (guitar) in tune! Let's begin.

There's more than one way to tune a guitar. In the beginning, it's easiest to use a guitar pitch pipe. When in tune, each string on the guitar produces a specific note that corresponds to one of the notes of the pitch pipe.

Here are some helpful hints.

Before starting to tune, experiment with your tuning pegs by turning them one way and then the other, to see which way tightens the string and which way loosens it. (Remember, tightening makes the pitch go *up*, loosening makes the pitch go *down*.) This will also help you to determine how much to turn the peg to get the pitch you want.

Try to keep your guitar in playing position while you are tuning up (see figure on page 7). You may have to lean forward or move the guitar to see which peg (also called tuning gear) is attached to which string, but after a while you will memorize the sequence. As a quick check, you can follow the string with a right hand finger down to its peg.

Blow a note on the pitch pipe. (The notes are marked on the pipe, corresponding to the open strings of the guitar – E A D G B E.) As you are blowing (and listening) pluck the corresponding string on the guitar and determine whether it is higher or lower than the note you are producing on the pipe. Turn the peg until the plucked string sounds the same as the sound of the pipe.

For those of you who are using a piano to tune your guitar, the 1st string on the guitar (high E) corresponds to the E above middle C. The low E string produces a sound two octaves below that. Here is a diagram which shows you how to find the notes you'll need on the piano.

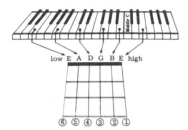

When tuning to the piano, hold down the sustaining pedal (the one on the right) with your foot. The note will ring longer, making it easier for you to match it up with the string you are tuning.

If you have neither pitch pipe nor piano, you can still get your guitar in tune. It's a little tricky, but definitely worth learning. There will be many times in the future that you'll have to tune your guitar without any other instruments around to tune to.

Start by assuming that the low E (6th string) is fairly on pitch. If it seems too high (tight) loosen the string a bit; if it seems too low (loose and buzzing) turn the peg to tighten the string a little.

When the 6th string sounds all right to you, fret it (press it down) on the fifth fret, using a left hand finger. At the same time, pluck that string with your right hand thumb or pick. The note you get will be an A, the correct note for the A (5th) string. Tune the 5th string to that sound.

When the 5th string is in tune with the 6th string, fret it at the 5th fret. This will give you the correct note to tune your D (4th) string to.

When that is in tune, fret it (the 4th string) at the 5th fret, and you'll get a G note. Tune the 3rd string to that note.

To tune the B (2nd string), press down the G string at the 4th fret. This will give you a B, so tune the 2nd string to that note.

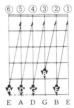

Finally, fret the 2nd string at the 5th fret to tune the 1st string. When you've done all that, play the two outer strings together. They should sound the same even though they are two octaves apart. Strum some of the chords you know to further check your tuning. You might have to go over your tuning a few times until you get the right sounds.

When you're playing in a group, you will tune your guitar to the other instruments in the band. If there is a piano or organ, everyone in the group will tune to that since it has a fixed pitch. Otherwise, choose the instrument that is closest to being perfectly in tune and use that as your standard. The nicest things can happen when several instruments get in tune and play together.

More Blues

Play this new chord with your tuned guitar:

G chord

If you can't manage the G chord using the 2nd, 3rd and 4th fingers, you'll find the fingering in parentheses much easier.

Practice changing from this new G chord to the D chord you already know. Once that feels pretty good to you, get into this blues progression in D.

Blues in D

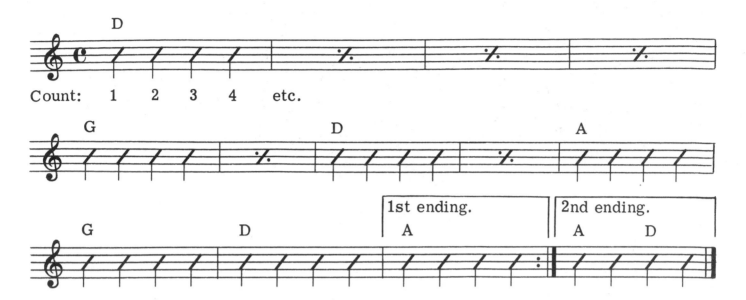

Count: 1   2   3   4   etc.

Only use the "2nd Ending" when you're finished playing the progression. For example if you repeat the entire progression four times, use the "1st Ending" the first three times through the progression. When you play through the progression the fourth and last time, use the "2nd Ending."

Now let's work on the rhythm of the blues progression. Up to this point you've been strumming the guitar once on each beat. Strum twice on each beat when you see two wedge-marks joined together by a bar.

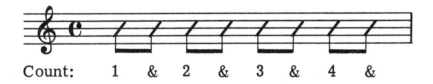

Count: 1   &   2   &   3   &   4   &

When you count, insert "&" between each beat to get a better feel for this new rhythm.

Play with a down-stroke of the pick ⊓ ⊓ on each beat and an up-stroke of the pick ∨ ∨ on each "&." If you keep the rhythm by tapping your foot, play a down-stroke when your foot taps the floor and an up-stroke when you raise it. Use the D chord for this exercise.

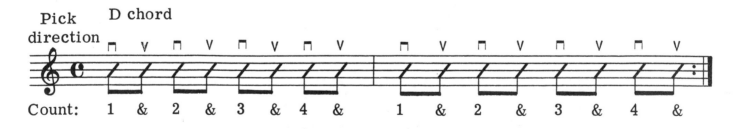

Count: 1   &   2   &   3   &   4   &   1   &   2   &   3   &   4   &

When you play the up-stroke, brush lightly just the first three strings or so with your pick. This techniques makes the up-strokes lighter in sound than the down-strokes, giving you a more solid beat. Play that last exercise again.

By using our new rhythm on beats 2 and 4, you create a very basic rock beat.

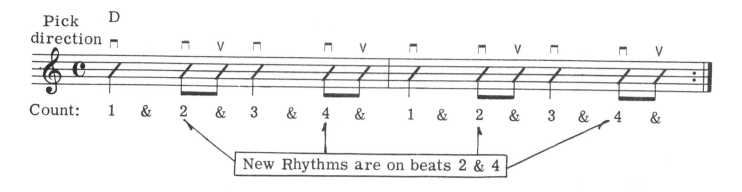

Pick direction

D

Count: 1 & 2 & 3 & 4 & 1 & 2 & 3 & 4 &

New Rhythms are on beats 2 & 4

Here is the D blues again with this new rock beat. Practice it until you can play it pretty fast—until it gives you a good feeling.

Blues in D

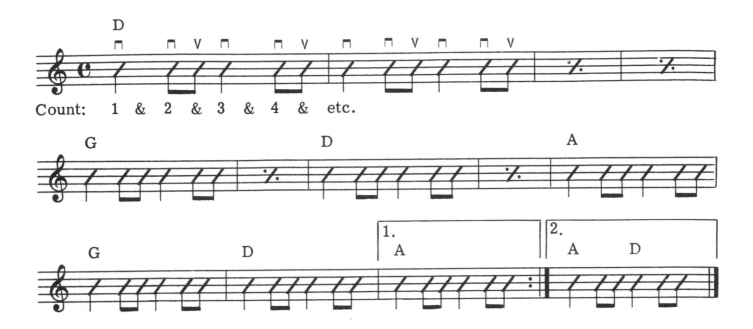

Count: 1 & 2 & 3 & 4 & etc.

As you can hear, these slight rhythmic variations definitely improve the flow of the progression. Apply the same rhythm to the *Blues in A*.

A new chord for a new progression:

C chord

Practice switching from this C chord to the G chord and back again. Now take a look at our next progression: *Blues in G*. A new rhythm occurs in the fourth measure—play one strum for each beat and two on the last beat. This also happens in measure eight and measure twelve. Play the progression through a few times on the slow side. Don't forget: once you start playing a piece, you must not slow down or speed up at any point. People are dancing so give them a steady beat.

Blues in G

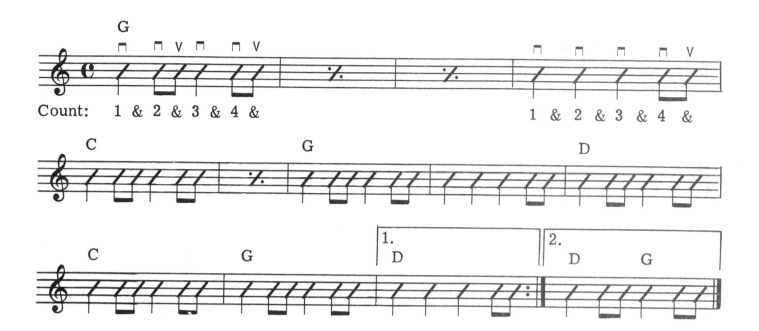

Here's a summary of the five chords you've learned up to this point. They should be "in your fingers" before continuing to the next lesson.

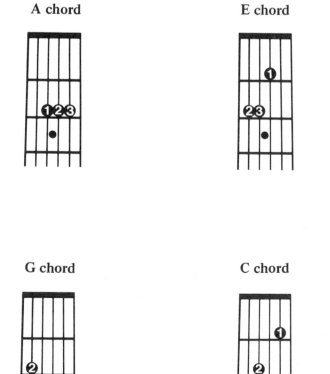

A chord

E chord

D chord

G chord

C chord

7th Chords

You're becoming a rock guitarist. The tuning is coming along and you know the five basic chords of rock 'n roll. Before leaving this introductory section, we'll take up a slightly more sophisticated chord: the dominant seventh.

For the E7* chord first finger the E chord you already know and then drop your pinky down on the 2nd string like so:

E7 chord

Set up a slow rhythm with the E chord and practice switching to the E7 and back again. Listen to the difference between the two chords. The E7 chord has a sort of tense feeling about it that the regular E chord doesn't have.

*Although the proper name for this chord is E dominant seventh, E7 is a standard abbreviation. Whenever you see an upper-case letter with a 7 (C7, A7, G7, etc.), you play a dominant seventh chord.

The same thing holds true for the A7 chord:

A7 chord

Try switching back and forth between the A chord and the A7 to better hear the difference.

On to a blues that makes use of our two new 7th chords. Be sure to get the pick directions and the rhythm changes right.

Blues in A

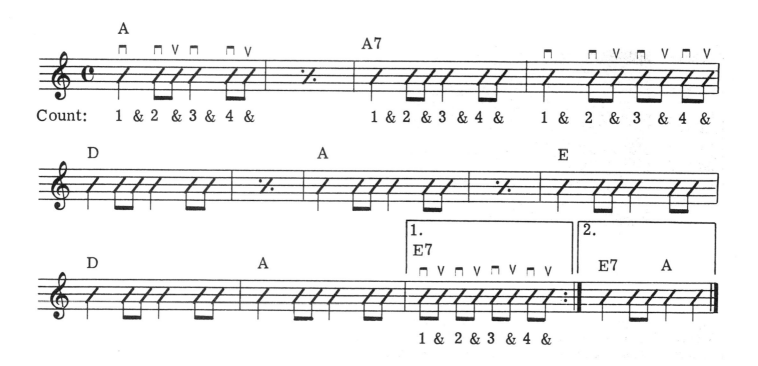

After you've played this blues a few times, go back and look at where the 7th chords occur. Notice that the use of the A7 in the third and fourth measures makes the change to the D chord in the fifth measure much more satisfying. Play the A7 and then the D chord and listen. The E7 to the A chord also sounds good. The increase in tension brought about by 7th chords makes the progression flow better.

A new 7th chord to learn:

G7 chord

When you're sure you have the right fingering, play this exercise using the G7. Keep your ears tuned-in, of course.

Most 7th chords are easy to get once you know the major chords. For example, to form the C7 chord, first finger the C chord and then drop your pinky down on the 3rd string.

C7 chord

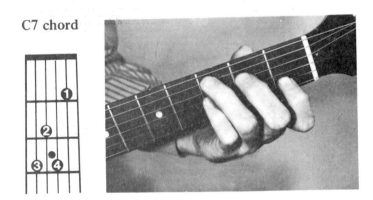

The D7 is easy, too. Remember not to play the 6th string.

D7 chord

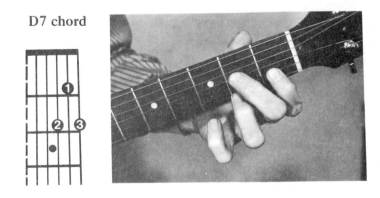

Here's a short progression that uses all the chords you've learned up to now.
You must know all ten of these chords.

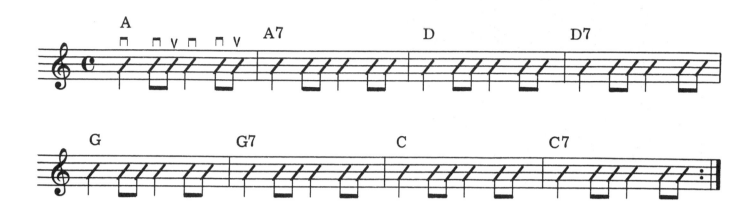

Your next song shows how you can liven up the blues progression by the frequent use of 7th chords. Play it many times. Hear how the 7th chords make the progression stick together better. Played at different speeds, the progression takes on new perspectives. Vary the speed until you discover one that expresses it best.

Blues in G

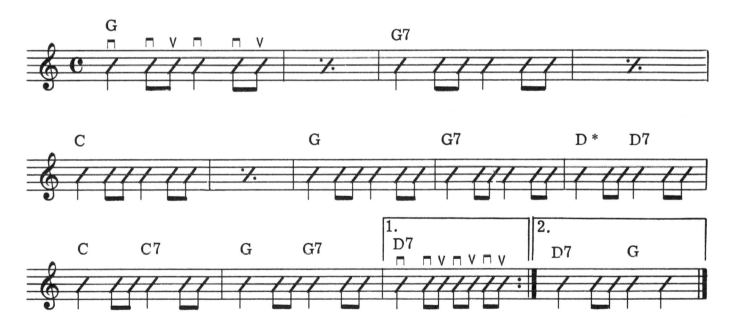

You are now finished with the introductory section. Why don't you reread the entire first section and make absolutely sure you understand it before you proceed to the next section? If you know the first section and you're sure of it, start immediately on Part II. Good luck!

*Using both D Major and D7 within the same measure adds interest to the progression. The next measure uses the same technique.

PART II
THE RHYTHM GUITARIST

Bar Chords

We are now going to take up the most important single technique of rhythm guitar: the bar chord. Carefully finger and play this F chord.

F chord

 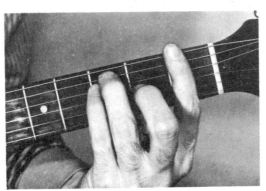

Don't be upset if the chord doesn't sound great the first time you try it. This is not an easy chord to finger. The 1st finger (which forms the *bar*) must be held straight as in the illustration.

Strum the chord very slowly starting with the 6th string. If any of the strings buzz or sound weak, check to see if you have the right fingering. If the fingering's right, then try pressing the bar down harder. Making bar chords is much easier if you use light-gauge strings on your guitar. The next

time you change strings put on a set of Fender Rock & Roll Light Gauge strings or Martin Flat-Wound Light-Gauge strings and you'll be amazed at how strong your fingers are.

Slide the entire chord formation up two frets (behind the 3rd fret). This gives you a G chord.

G chord

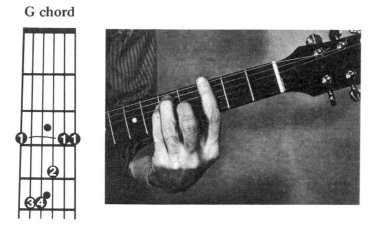

This gives you two ways of making a G chord: a bar G chord and an *open* G chord. (*Open* refers to the fact that you used open or unfingered strings to form the chord.)

As soon as you feel comfortable playing the G and F bar chords, play this *Blues in C*. Remember to keep the rhythm constant. (*Must* I remind you?) Check the footnotes if you have trouble making any of the chord changes.

Blues in C

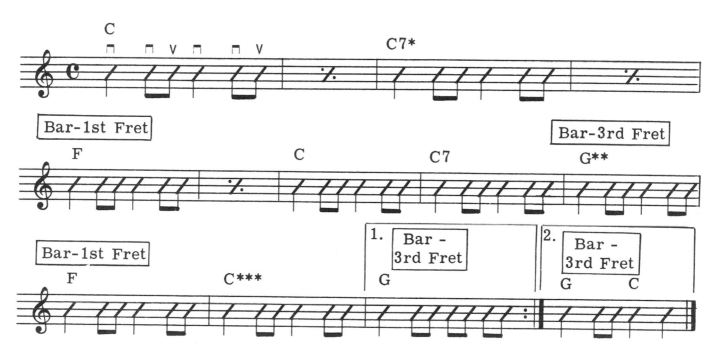

*After you've finished playing the C7, lift up all the fingers of the left hand *except* the 3rd finger. This puts the 3rd finger in position for the F chord. Always try to leave at least one left hand finger in contact with the fingerboard.

**When you're ready to switch from the G chord to the F chord, pick up the bar and slide the rest of the major chord position down two frets.

***When changing from the C chord to the G chord, pick up all your left hand fingers except the 3rd. Then slide the 3rd finger up two frets and position the G chord.

NOTES PRODUCED
BY THE 6TH STRING

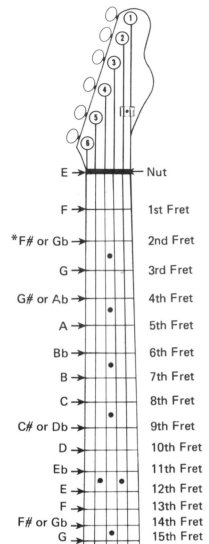

E →	Nut
F →	1st Fret
*F# or Gb →	2nd Fret
G →	3rd Fret
G# or Ab →	4th Fret
A →	5th Fret
Bb →	6th Fret
B →	7th Fret
C →	8th Fret
C# or Db →	9th Fret
D →	10th Fret
Eb →	11th Fret
E →	12th Fret
F →	13th Fret
F# or Gb →	14th Fret
G →	15th Fret

Now for some theory.

This next illustration indicates every note the 6th string produces. Play and name each note on the 6th string all the way up to the 12th fret and back down a few times. Although it's actually a good idea to know all the notes produced by the 6th string, you can get by if you'll remember that at the 1st fret the 6th string produces F, at the 3rd fret G, the 5th fret A, the 7th B, and the 8th fret C.

F chord

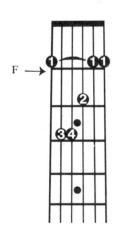

F →

Fact: each chord has in it a tone from which the chord gets its name. This tone is called the *root* of the chord. In the bar chord that you know, the root is on the 6th string. So if you wanted to make an F chord, you would first locate F on the 6th string (1st fret) and then make the bar chord behind that fret.

*# is a sharp. Sharps are one fret *higher* on the fingerboard than a note of the same letter name. For example, F is on the 1st fret of the 6th string whereas F# is on the 2nd fret. b is a flat. Flats are one fret *lower* on the fingerboard than a note of the same letter name. For example, A is on the 5th fret of the 6th string while Ab is on the 4th fret. (Yes, G# and Ab are the same note.)

A chord

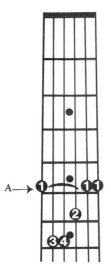

To make an A chord simply locate A on the 6th string (5th fret) and make the bar chord behind that fret.

With just the knowledge of this one bar chord and the notes the 6th string produces, you can play all eleven major chords (from E all the way up to Eb). Play this *Blues in F* using only bar chords. If your left hand gets very tired, stop and relax it for a minute or so rather than going on. Try not to push the strings down with the left hand any harder than you have to.

Blues in F

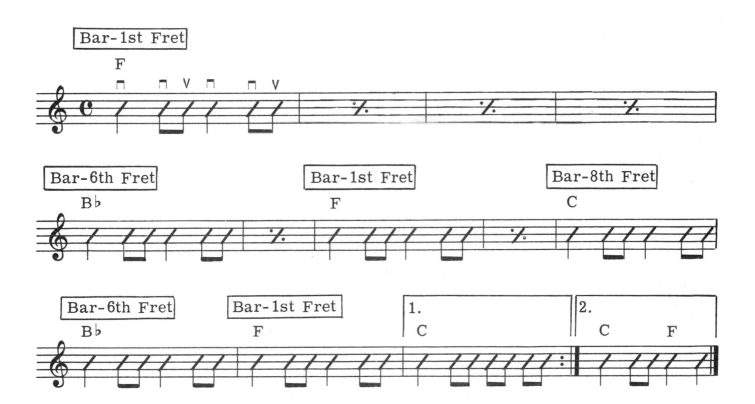

Make sure this blues sounds groovy before proceeding to the next lesson.

Special Effects

After that last lesson, you're entitled to an easy lesson. With your knowledge of the bar chord, you can easily play many of the special effects that rhythm guitar players use. One of the more frequently used effects is the staccato strum.

The whole idea of the staccato strum is to make the total sound of the chord stop an instant after it is sounded. It's really quite easy. First, finger the A chord at the 5th fret (bar chord). Strum the A chord with a brisk down-stroke of the pick and as soon as the chord is sounded, relax the fingers of the left hand *leaving them in contact with the strings*. The staccato strum is indicated by a dot over the wedge-mark: $\overset{\cdot}{/}$. Let's try a few.

Make the A chord and set up a slow, one strum to the beat rhythm. Once you get it going, switch into the staccato chord.

Remember to leave the left hand fingers on the strings.

Turn the treble up all the way on your amplifier (if you are using one) to give the staccato strum a crisper sound. (Use the super-treble or the treble booster if your amp has one.) If you have reverb in your amp, turn it on and set the dial about in the middle to give depth to the staccato strum.

Just to make sure you understand how to play the staccato strum, go through the last blues we worked on (page 27) but this time play four staccato strums in each measure. In many rock tunes the rhythm guitarist only plays staccato strums like this* so get a good feel for them.

---

*The Beatles' *A Little Help From My Friends* from the album *Sgt. Pepper's Lonely Hearts Club Band* is a fine example.

Rather than simply playing a staccato strum on each beat, alternate the staccato strum with the regular method of strumming for a more professional sound. Play a staccato strum on beats 2 and 4, and the regular strum on beats 1 and 3. This will give you a sort of pulsating rhythm that is very effective for dancing.

Count: 1   2   3   4   1   2   3   4

          (Staccato)   (Staccato)   (Staccato)   (Staccato)

The next *Blues in G* uses the same pulsating rhythm. Work on this progression carefully as this method of strumming is very popular. Strive for a flowing rhythm. Use all bar chords, and refer to page 26 if you don't remember where they're located.

Blues in G

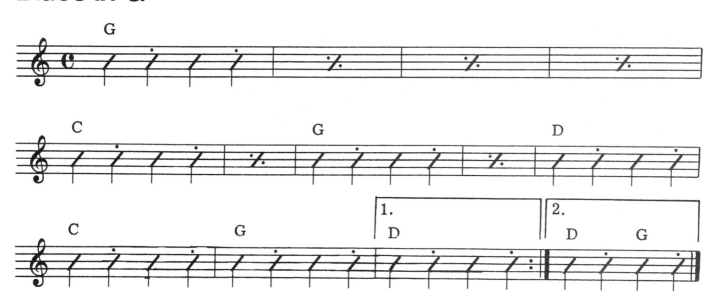

An accent mark >   >   above a chord means that you play it louder than the other chords in the same measure. The drive of a song is greatly increased if you accent the staccato strum. Try it.

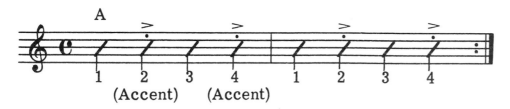

1   2   3   4   1   2   3   4

(Accent)   (Accent)

To further increase the drive, play only the 4th, 5th, and 6th strings on beats 1 and 3. This makes the staccato strum stand out more. Try this:

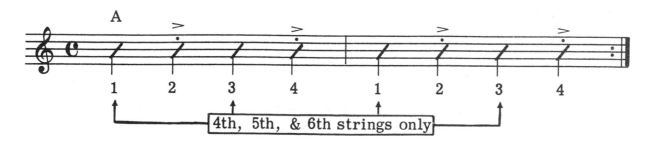

Go back to the last *Blues in G* that we did. Take it again but this time at a pretty fast speed. By accenting the staccato strums, notice how much more exciting the progression becomes.

Still another type of strum that will make your playing more interesting is the percussive strum. Because you know the staccato strum, this strum will be a snap to learn. Here's how you do it:

First, make the A chord at the 5th fret again. Now start a slow, one strum to the beat rhythm. Once you get it going, relax the fingers of the left hand leaving them in contact with the strings while you continue to strum. The resulting sound is called a percussive strum as it has no definite pitch. This chord is indicated by an x on the wedge-mark:  .

What you were playing looks like this:

30

Actually, these two methods of strumming a chord work quite well together. In the next exercise, play the staccato strum on the down-beat and the percussive strum on the up-beat (up-stroke). When you make the up-stroke of the pick to play the percussive strum, only play the first three or four strings.

Combining this method of strumming with the normal method, the sound becomes even more interesting.

Play this *Blues in F* using all bar chords. Use the new method of strumming accenting the staccato strums on beats 2 and 4 and playing only the lower strings on beats 1 and 3 (wow).

Blues in F

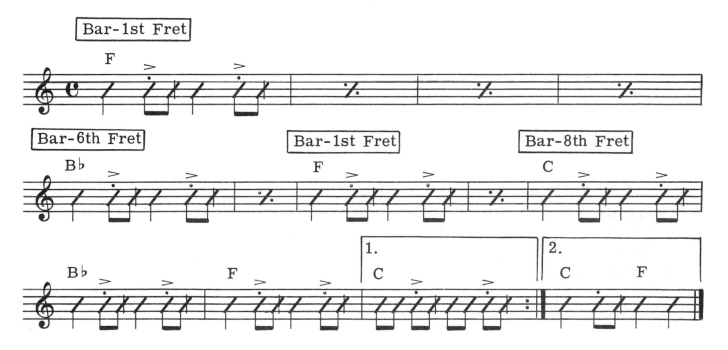

Another strumming effect very much like the percussive strum is the open-string chord. With this chord you strum the first two or three strings open (unfingered) with an up-stroke of the pick. A small o above the wedge-mark indicates the open chord:

Try it:

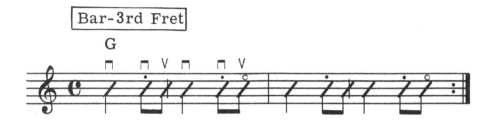

Because you are not touching the strings when you play this chord, your hand is free to advance to another chord position. The open-string chord, then, is quite useful when changing chords as it gives your left hand a few seconds of freedom to finger a new chord.

To end this lesson play *Blues in G* using bar chords, percussive and staccato strums, open-string chords, and accents.

Blues in G

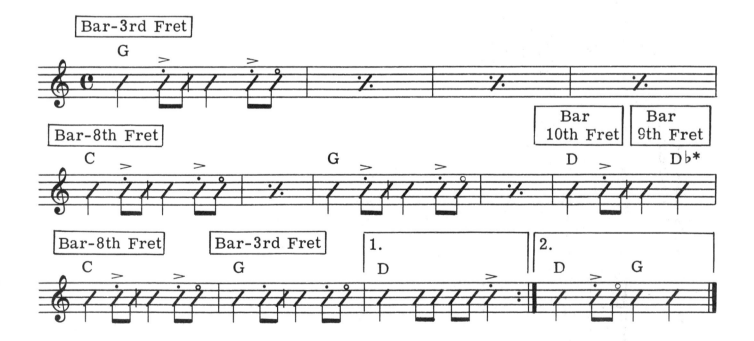

Inserting the Db chord here serves to connect the C and D chords.

More Bar Chords

Announcing another important bar chord! Finger and play this Bb chord.

Bb chord

Bb chord alternate

Strum the chord very slowly and listen to each string. If the 1st string sounds weak, check and see if the 3rd finger is touching it at any point. Light-gauge strings make this 3rd finger bar much easier. If you can't manage the chord with this fingering, here's an alternate fingering.

Slide this bar chord up two frets (behind the third fret) and you have a C chord:

C chord

After you can play both the C and the Bb chords, try this *Blues in F*.

Blues in F

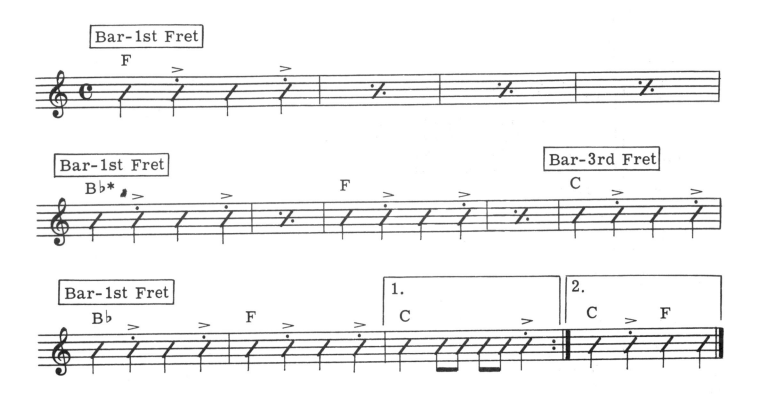

The top-ranking rock guitarists would play the above progression with the same choice of staccato and bar strums. Work on that blues until it really swings.

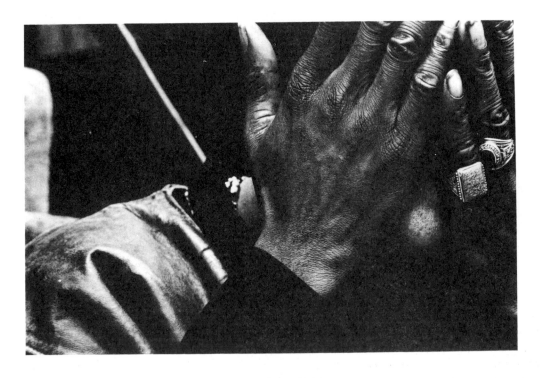

*When you switch from the F bar chord to the Bb bar chord, keep the 1st finger (the bar) in place. Only change the position of the remaining fingers.

NOTES PRODUCED
BY THE 5TH STRING

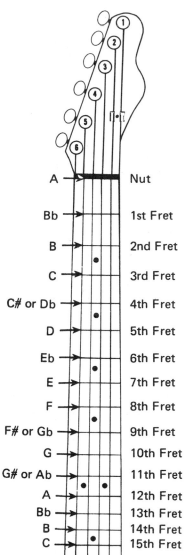

And some theory for this new bar chord:

The root of this chord is on the 5th string so it's a good idea to know the notes produced by that string. Look over this illustration and play the notes and name them a few times.

To locate a chord using this bar chord position, first find the note on the 5th string and then make the bar chord at that fret. D, for example, is found at the 5th fret of the 5th string. So this new bar chord at the 5th fret produces a D chord:

Try locating and playing a few other chords with this bar chord. Can you locate an E chord and play it? An F chord? How about a G chord? Very good. Play this next progression using only this new bar chord. Naturally all the special effects you have learned, such as the percussive strum, the staccato strum, and the open-string chord work with this bar chord as well as the first one you learned.

35

Progression

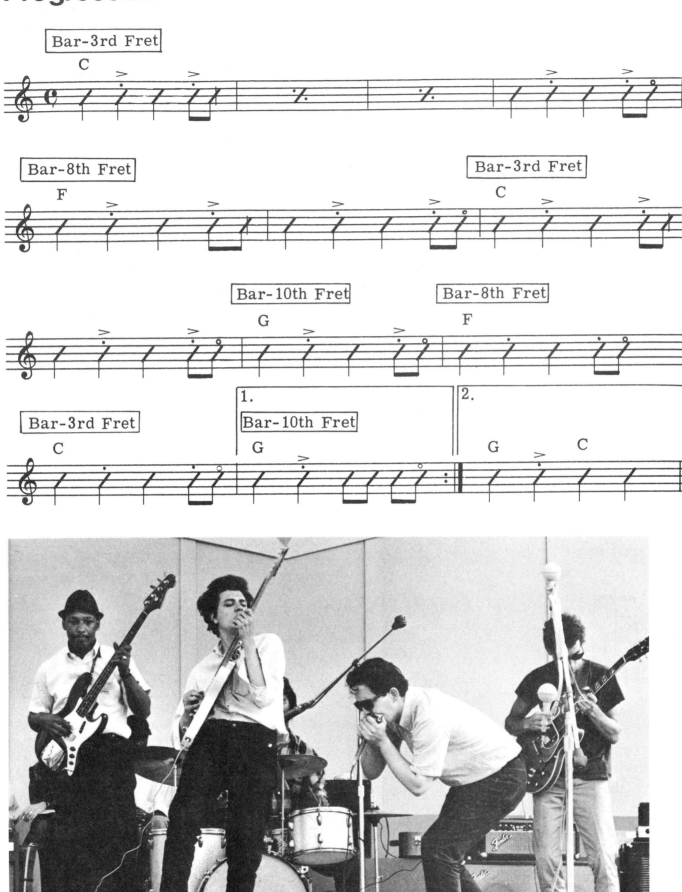

Skull Practice

Up to this point you've learned two bar chords: a bar chord with its root on the 6th string and the one we just finished learning with its root on the 5th string. The first chord we'll call the *root 6 bar chord* and the second the *root 5 bar chord*. Most rhythm guitar playing is done with these two bar chords.

By combining the *root 6 bar chord* with the *root 5 bar chord*, the blues progression is much easier to play. Try this one in G. Keep the same bar at the 3rd fret for the first eight measures.

Blues in G

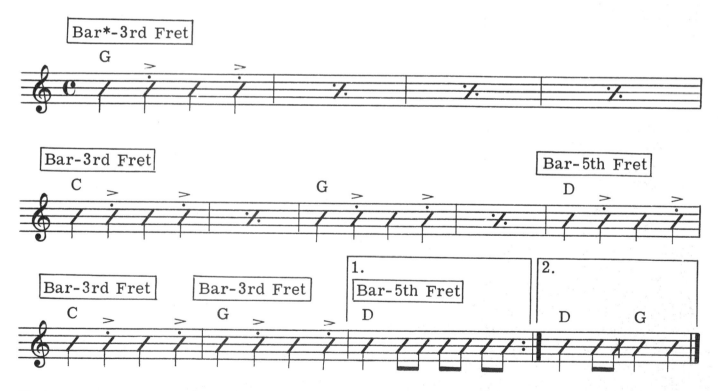

Notice that the hand position only changes twice: once in the 9th measure and once in the 12th measure. This is the way professionals play a standard rock progression.

*The bar indication tells you which bar chord to use. A G chord at the 3rd fret could only be a *root 6 bar chord*.

Armed with the knowledge of these two bar chords, you can now play the blues chord progression in any key. First, play a *root 6 bar chord* in the key of the blues for the first four measures; next, go to a *root 5 bar chord* at the same fret for two measures; then, back to the first chord for two more measures—altogether this makes eight measures. In the ninth measure the bar is moved up two frets for a *root 5 bar chord*; the tenth measure is the *root 5 bar chord* in the original bar position; the eleventh measure is the original *root 6 bar chord*; and the twelfth measure is the *root 5 bar chord* up two frets again. Then, back to the beginning . . . .

Try it again.

Standard Progression

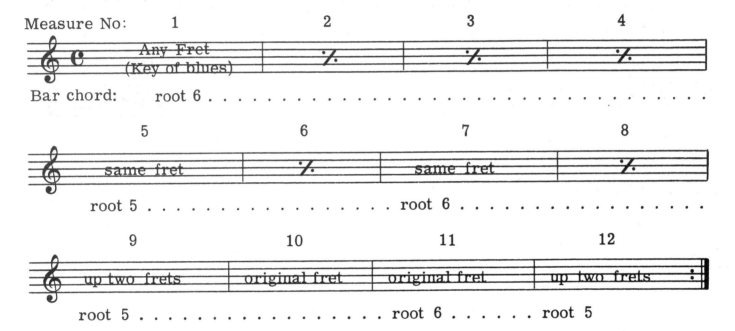

Compare this outline with the *Blues in G* that you did in this lesson.

So say you're playing somewhere and the guitar player turns to you and says, "Let's play *Green Onions**." "A blues progression?" you ask. He tells you it is, and that he wants to play it in the key of A. So you find A on the 6th string (5th fret), make a *root 6 bar chord* at that fret, and play the progression following the outline. Just to make sure you understand this, play the standard blues progression in the following keys using any strum that you want and at any speed you desire.

  1) In the key of F (starting at the 1st fret)
  2) The key of A (starting at the 5th fret)
  3) The key of Bb (6th fret)
  4) The key of B (7th fret)
  5) The key of C (8th fret)

In order to avoid starting the progression at an uncomfortably high fret (say the 10th or 11th fret), you can start the progression with the *root 5 bar chord*. This is an alternate way of playing the standard progression.

Green Onions is a very popular instrumental number using the blues progression. A marvelous rendition of this tune can be found on the album *Back to Back, The Mar-keys & Booker T. & the MG's* (Stax 720). The tasteful rhythm and lead guitar work of Steve Cropper on this album is quite instructive.

Standard Progression

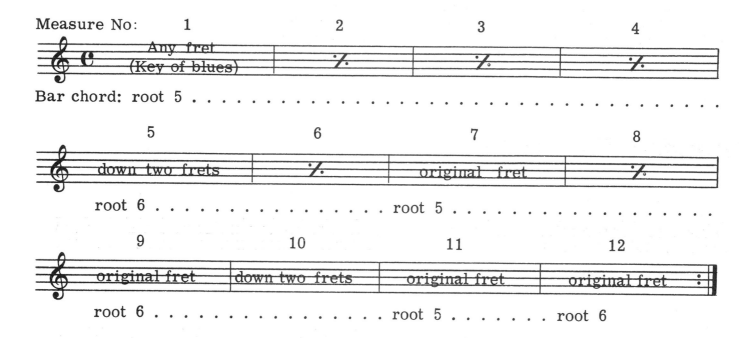

Here's the progression C. Play it and compare it to the above outline.

Blues in C

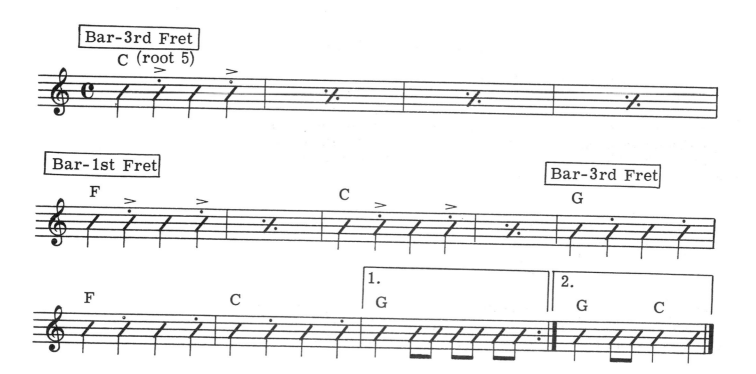

Play the progression in D (5th fret) and E (7th fret) starting with the *root 5 bar chord.*

Bar 7th Chords

Both the bar chords you've learned can easily be turned into 7th chords. Any *root 6 bar chord* can be made into a 7th chord by simply moving the 4th finger to the 2nd string:

F7 chord

Strum this chord a few times making sure all the strings are sounding. Play it at a few different frets. This 7th chord has the same letter name as the *root 6 bar chord* and you locate it the same way:

G7 at the 3rd fret   and A7 at the 5th fret.

Here's a little exercise to play using this new 7th chord. The quarter note rest is introduced here for the first time: ⸽ . When you see this rest sign, do not play for one beat. This will be clearer in the exercise.

Exercise

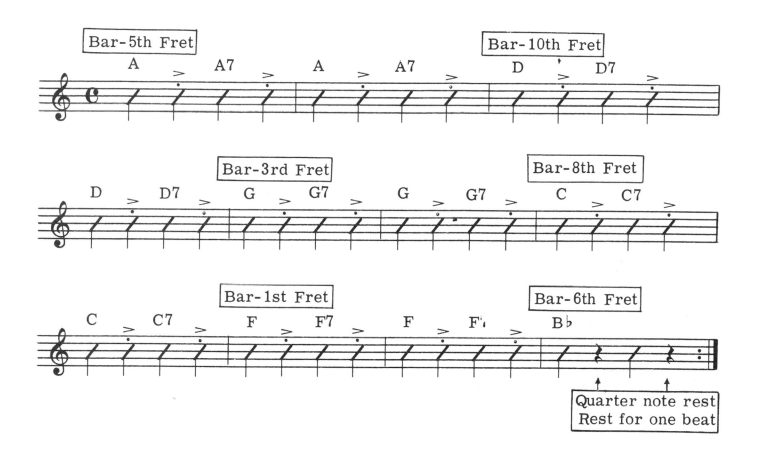

Quarter note rest
Rest for one beat

To make the *root 5 bar chord* into a 7th chord is even simpler. Put the pinky down like so to turn the Bb chord into a Bb 7th chord:

Bb7 chord

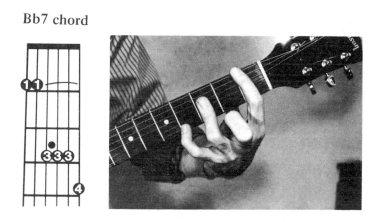

Play this 7th chord at other frets and listen carefully making sure it sounds clear. This 7th chord has the same letter name as the *root 5 bar chord*, and you locate it the same way. Try this exercise.

Exercise

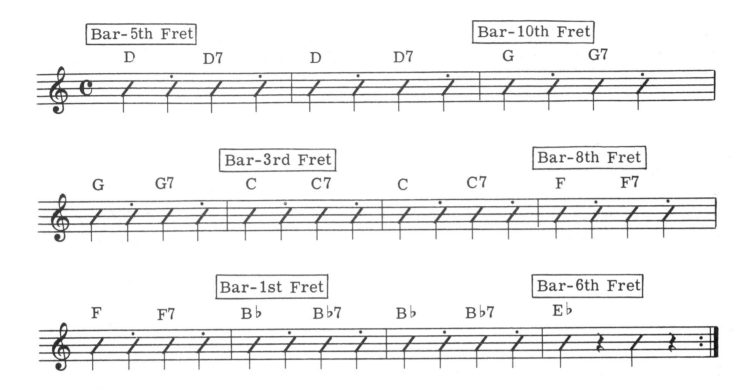

Now to a great exercise that illustrates how these two 7th chords work together. Work on this exercise until you can play it at a pretty fast speed, and you'll gain much better pick control. Try moving only your wrist using light but firm strokes of the pick.

If your left hand becomes tired, rest for a few seconds and then go on. Practice it about fifteen minutes a day for a couple of weeks.

Exercise

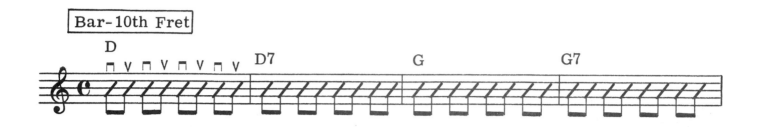

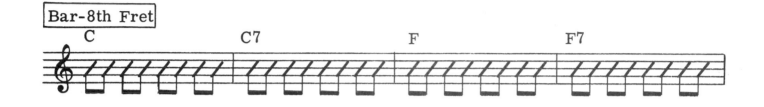

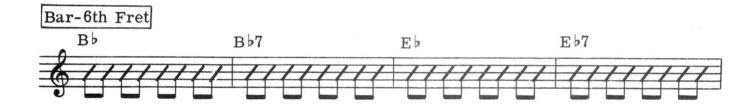

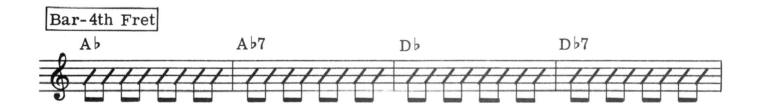

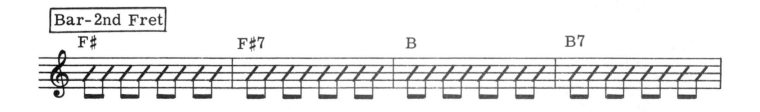

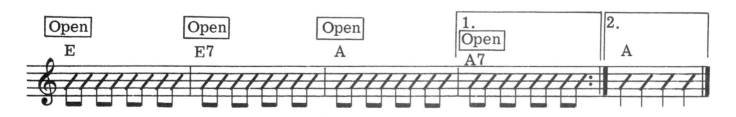

And here's how these new 7th chords work in the blues progression. Play
and listen.

Progression in G

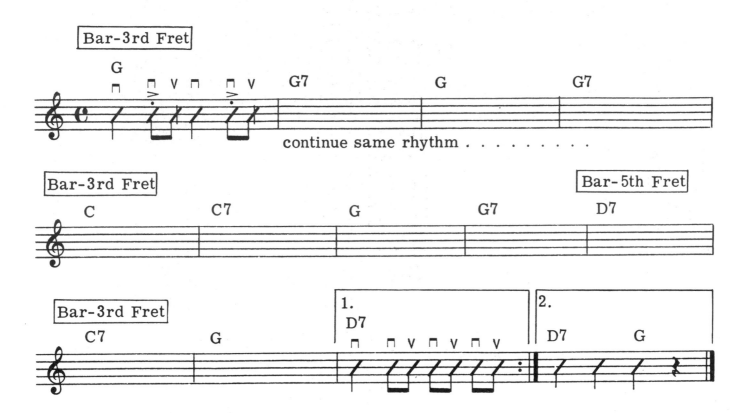

Without the 7th chords, this progression is identical to the outline on page
37. 7th chords are used to add interest to chord progressions. More about
this later.

One last 7th chord to learn. Remember the C7 chord from *PART ONE*?
Form that chord again but this time let your 1st finger (holding down the
2nd string) lightly touch the 1st string and your left hand thumb (coming
over the top of the neck) lightly touch the 6th string.

C7 chord (using thumb)

*The x's on the 1st and 6th strings indicate that the sound from these two strings is
to be deadened.*

Like the *root 5 bar chord*, the root of this new 7th chord is on the 5th string. The 3rd finger of the left hand gives you the letter name of the chord.

With this chord at the 3rd fret, the 3rd finger produces D so the chord is a D7 chord.

Or at the 5th fret you have an E7.

D7 chord (using thumb)   **E7 chord (using thumb)**

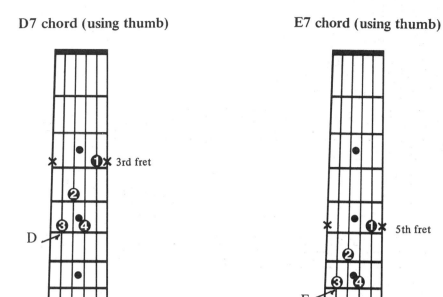

Play this *Blues in A* using the new 7th chord. The rhythm of the progression suggests that the drummer is taking a solo.

Blues in A

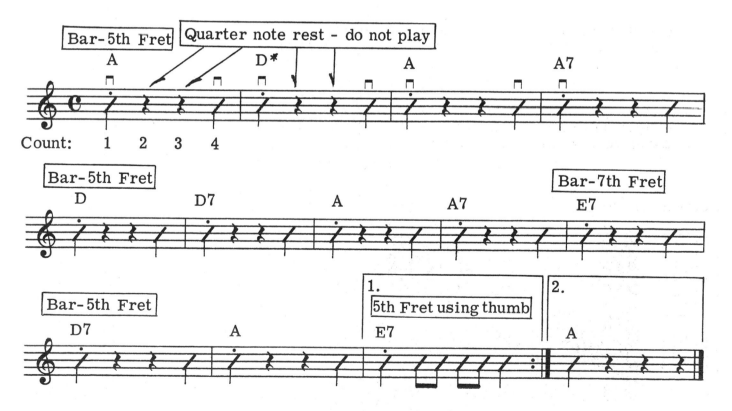

*Using the chord from the 4th measure of the blues progression in the 2nd measure is a popular way to add interest to the progression.

It's a little awkward going from the new E7 chord (1st ending) back to the A chord so many guitarists use an alternate fingering here for the A chord. Play the new E7 chord again and then switch to the A chord using this fingering.

A chord

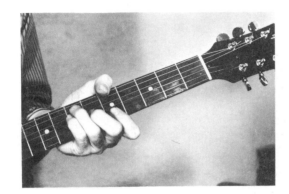

The 1st string remains deadened with this way of fingering the major chord. The thumb however presses down on the 6th string as illustrated.

Take the *Blues in A* again using the alternate fingering for the A chord the second time through the progression.

New Progressions

You know all the basic major chords and the very important standard blues progression. With the more than 60 chords you know, you are now equipped to play a large number of rock tunes.

By this time you should start learning some of the songs that use the blues progression. Check *APPENDIX* A on page 126 for any albums under *traditional rhythm 'n blues* or *blues bands* that you might own or could buy or borrow. Almost all the tunes on the albums in these two categories uses the blues progression that you know. Pick out a few of the tunes and start learning them. The first thing you have to do with a song that uses the blues progression is figure out the key that it's in. As a rule, the first chord in the song (and the last chord) tells you the key of the progression. Once you figure out the key of the song, use the formula for the standard progression and play along with the record. For example, in the Slim Harpo album *Rainin' in my Heart,"* the tune *Moody Blues* starts on an F chord and uses the standard progression in F following the outline. However, if you listen to a song and you can't figure out what key it's in, the song probably uses a variation of the blues progression so skip it. Try to pick songs that use only the standard progression that we've studied. You'll find that the rhythms used in these tunes are quite varied so play the song over many times and try to fall into the "feel" of the tune. We'll get into more complicated rhythms very shortly. Pick out a few of the tunes that you like that use the standard progression and try singing and playing the song without using the record. Although these tunes are not from the top ten of the day, millions of people have crowded into theatres and night clubs to hear them played.

There are many other popular chord progressions that are very similar to the blues progression, and we'll take up some of those now. These progressions won't give you any trouble since they use the same chords and have the same flavor as the standard blues progression. This first progression should be played on the fast side.

Rock Progression #1

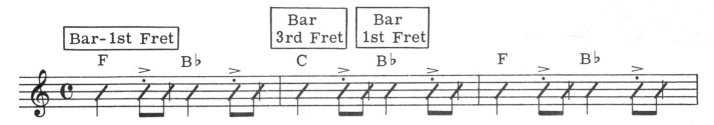

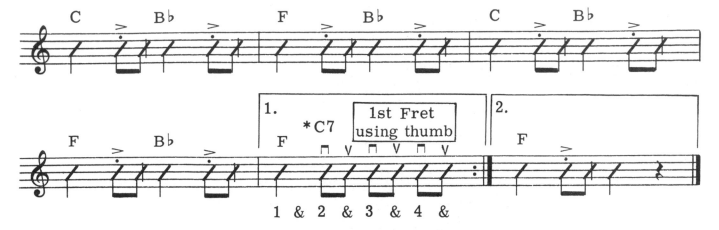

The rhythm of a progression is made much more interesting by the use of the tie: ⌢ When two wedge-marks are tied together, play only the first one. In the example below you do *not* play on the 4th beat.

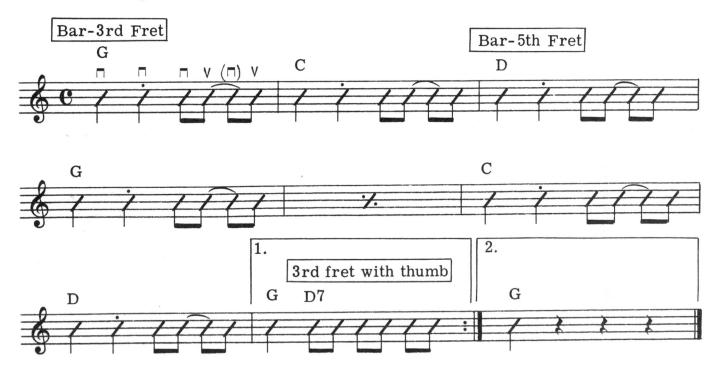

Notice that even though you don't actually sound the chord on the 4th beat, you still move the pick in a down-stroke (⊓) but above the strings. This prepares you for the up-stroke on the "&."

Play this new progression using the tie. Practice this progression until you can play it at a fast speed.

Rock Progression #2

*The 7th chord comes on the 2nd beat here so be careful.

Playing chords slightly ahead of the beat is another popular method of accompanying songs. This is called syncopation. To better understand it, first play this example. Be careful not to play on beats 2 and 3.

Keeping the same strumming pattern with the right hand, change to an E chord on the "&" after the 2nd beat.

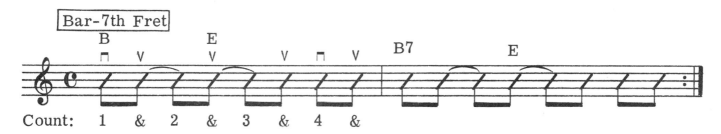

So instead of playing the E chord on the 3rd beat, you play it right before the beat. This is syncopation. Here's a progression to play using this same syncopated rhythm. Both the chord progression and rhythm are frequently used in rock tunes so really master this one. Start by practicing the progression quite slowly and gradually speed it up.

Rock Progression#3

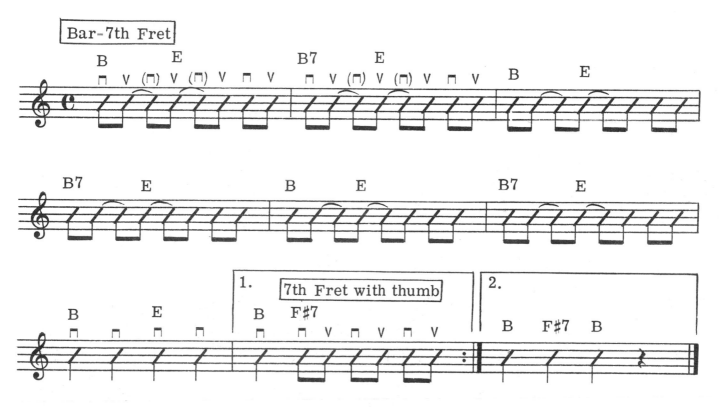

Play this progression for an ever so slight variation. The staccato strums and open-string chords add much to the drive of the rhythm. As always, start by playing the progression slowly and once you get it, speed up.

Rock Progression #4

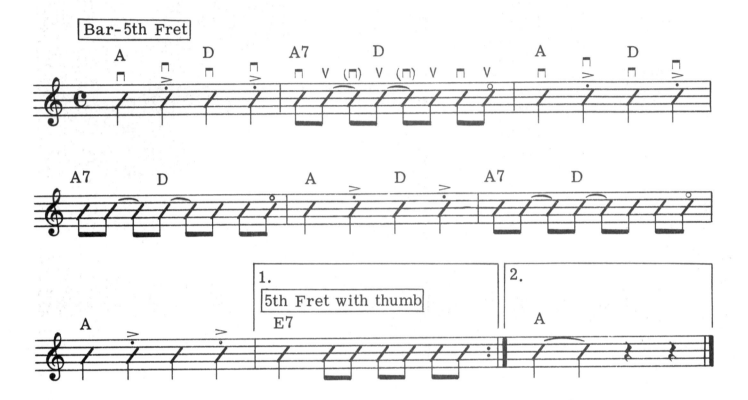

As you begin to see, the variations possible with these two basic bar chords are numerous. Listen to any rock radio station that plays the top fifty or so rock tunes and try to pick out some of the tunes that sound similar to the progressions we've been working on. Make a list of these type of tunes and the next time you go to a music store, buy the sheet music for a couple of them and learn them. The sheet music will have the words with the chord symbols above words. Frequently, chord diagrams appear beside the chords symbols to illustrate where and how you play the chords. Ignore these diagrams and use the bar chords we've been working with. If you can't get the sheet music, buy the song on a 45 record and learn off of that. The more songs you learn, the better off you're going to be.

An interesting and easy way to come up with new rhythms is to first start playing any of the progressions we've worked on so far. Keep playing the progression over and over at the same speed (if you have a metronome, use it) and eventually new ideas will suggest themselves to you. When you think of a new rhythm figure, use it. Keep trying to make the rhythm more and more interesting. Do anything with the rhythm that you think adds to the movement or the interest. One very important thing to remember is to keep the speed the same. If you do this exercise for about 15 minutes a day for a week, you'll be amazed at how much more you know about rhythms and how much better your *feel* for rhythm guitar is.

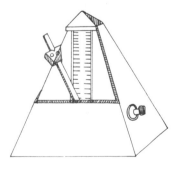

Minor Chords

Now we'll get into a different quality of rock 'n roll chords: the minor chord. Strum this A minor chord very slowly and listen for the empty, melancholy sound that characterizes minor chords.

Am chord *

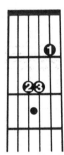

Compare the sound on the A minor chord to that of the A major chord you learned in *PART ONE*.

A chord

Notice that the only physical difference is that the tone produced by the 2nd string is altered by one fret. But that one fret suggests a completely different world.

---

*Minor chords are abbreviated by placing a small *m* next to the letter name of the chord.

One of the more common uses of the minor chord is in the rock 'n roll "turn around." The turn around progression was very popular in the 50's and is modestly popular today. Songs that use the turn around are usually played at slow speeds. Here's how it sounds in the key of C. Use open* chords unless otherwise indicated.

Turn Around in C

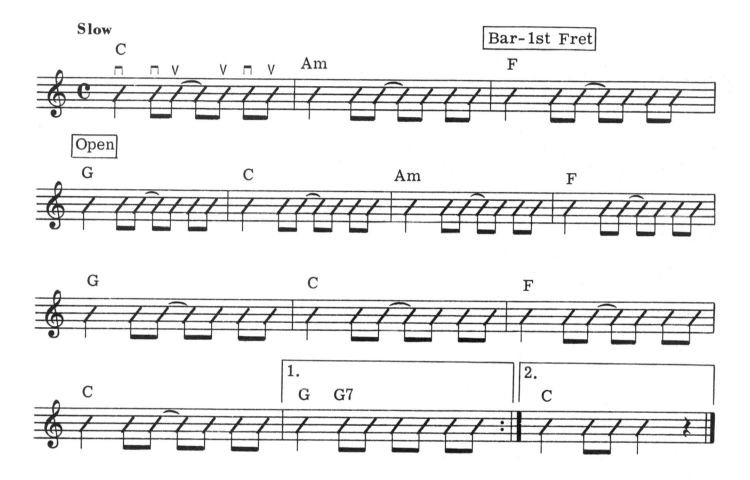

I'm sure the turn around sounds pretty familiar to you. Below is the E minor chord. Play it and compare it to the E chord. By merely raising the 1st finger of the left hand, you convert the E major chord into the E minor chord.

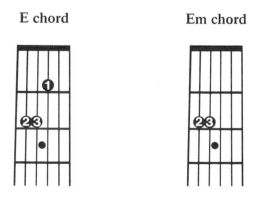

E chord   Em chord

*Chords with unfingered strings like you learned in *PART ONE*.

In order to give the turn around a more professional sound, some guitarists play a single string at each chord change. For example with the G chord, you would first finger the chord and then play the 6th string. This would be indicated by the number of the string to be played just below the wedge-mark.

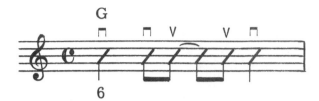

Play only the 6th string on the 1st beat with your regular strumming for the rest of the bar.

A turn around with this technique:

Turn Around in G

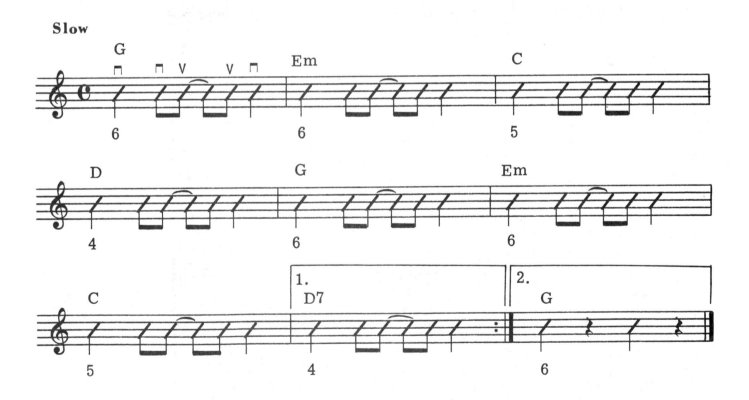

When you hear the bass guitar playing a bass-note pattern similar to the one used in the last progression, you can almost bet that the progression is a turn around. When you're listening to a rock song and trying to figure out the chords, this is the type of thing you listen for.

D minor is another important minor chord to learn. Compare the sound and the fingering to the D major chord. Avoid playing the 6th string with both of these chords.

D chord   **Dm chord**

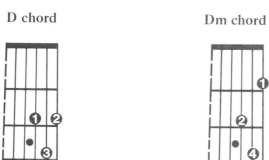

The next turn around uses the triplet rhythm. This is not a difficult rhythm to understand but you'll have to read carefully. The idea of the triplet rhythm is to play three evenly spaced chords (or notes) on one beat. Wedge-marks joined together in groups of three 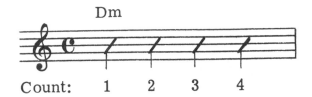 indicate this rhythm.

To get the feel of playing triplets, first play this measure counting the beats:

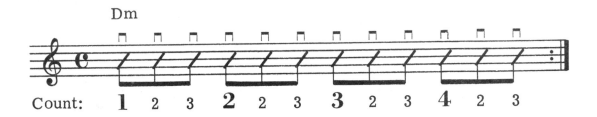

Count: 1   2   3   4

Rather than counting one number for each beat, add a *2* and *3* after each count: **1** 2 3 **2** 2 3 **3** 2 3 **4** 2 3 . Each beat should have a distinct feeling of three. Try it with the Dm chord. Notice the pick plays only in down-strokes.

Play this example many times. It should be slow and smooth.

Now try this turn around.

Turn Around in F

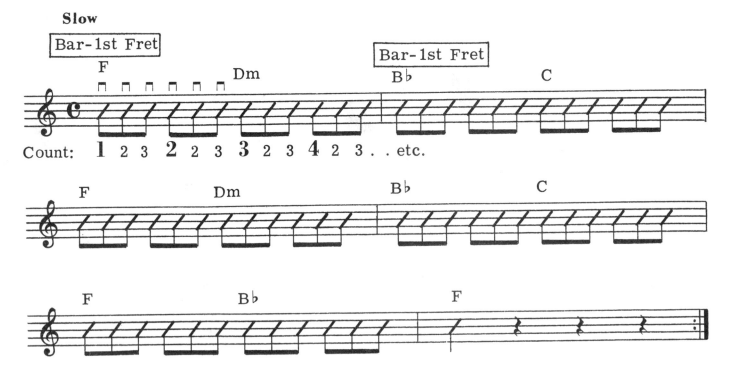

Another popular way of playing the turn around is to combine the triplet rhythm with single string playing. In this next turn around, play a single string *on* the chord change as before, and also *before* the chord change. This will become clear as you play.

Turn Around in C

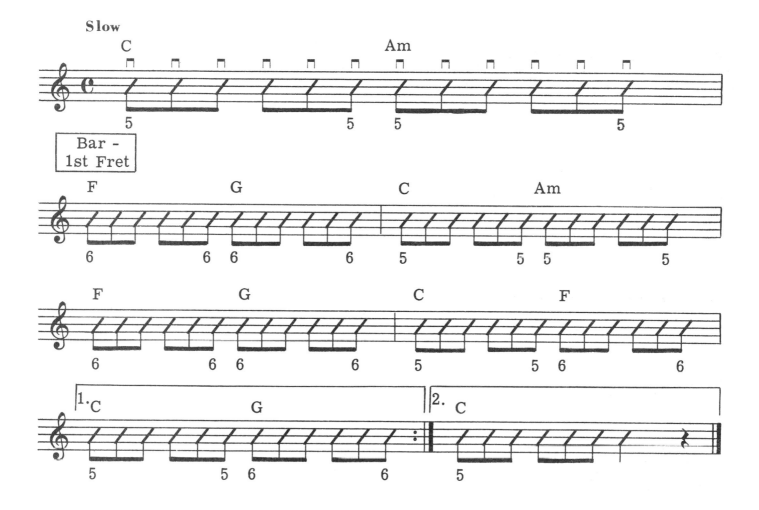

After this turn around sounds good, go back and play the *Turn Around in G* using triplets and playing single strings on and before the chord changes.

New Bar Chords

What do you think happens when you have to play a turn-around in some other key than C, G, or F? Right! You have to use bar chords. The minor bar chords are similar to the major bar chords, and they shouldn't give you any trouble.

Make the F chord that you know behind the 1st fret.

F chord

Pick up the 2nd finger and you have an F minor chord.

Fm chord

Both of these chords are *root 6 bar chords* so the position of the bar gives you the letter name of both the major chord *and* the minor chord.

When the bar is behind the third fret you have:

either a **G chord**   or a **Gm chord**

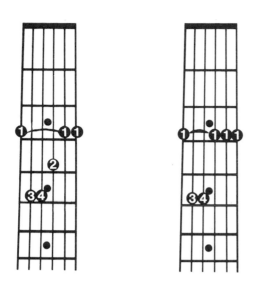

All you have to remember is the notes the 6th string produces (page 26).
Try this turn around using this new minor bar chord.

Turn Around in Bb

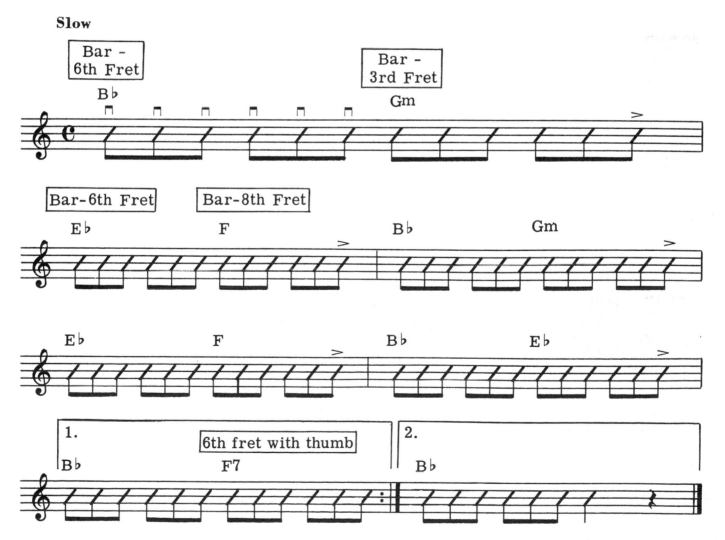

I hope you noticed the accent marks (>) and strummed a little louder when you saw them. If you forgot to, then go back and play the turn around again.

To learn another important minor bar chord make the Bb chord at the 1st fret:

Bb chord

Now refinger that chord and lower the 2nd string one fret:

Bbm chord

This new minor bar chord is a *root 5 bar chord* so wherever the bar is on the 5th string gives you the letter name of the chord. At the 3rd fret you have a C minor chord, at the 5th fret a D minor chord, at the 7th fret an E minor chord, etc. Just remember the notes the 5th string produces (page 35).

We'll take up a progression with this minor bar chord after you learn a new strum. Back to the triplet rhythm we've been working with. Instead of counting 1 2 3 2 2 3 3 2 3 4 2 3 like you've been doing, insert an "&" between each number like so:

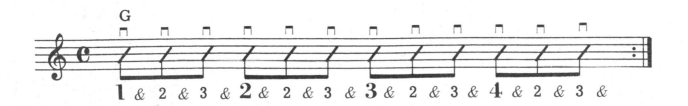

Play the example and count out loud a few times.

Still counting, insert a brisk up-stroke of the pick on the "&" between 2 and 3. Try it.

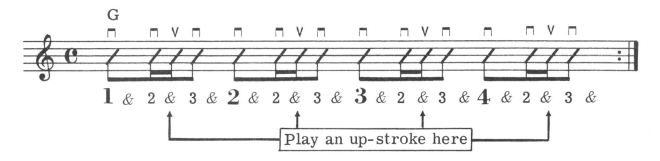

Keep working on this new rhythm until you can play it smoothly at a moderate speed. Use a light and brisk strum without holding the pick too firmly.

With the straight triplet rhythm on beats 2 and 4, play 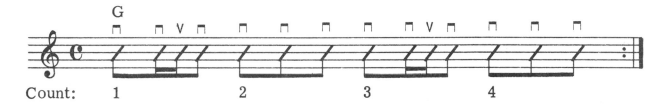 our new rhythm on beats 1 and 3. This really sounds nice on the guitar.

Practice this strum quite slowly until it holds together well. Try it on this new progression that also uses the minor *root 5 bar chord*.

Turn Around in D

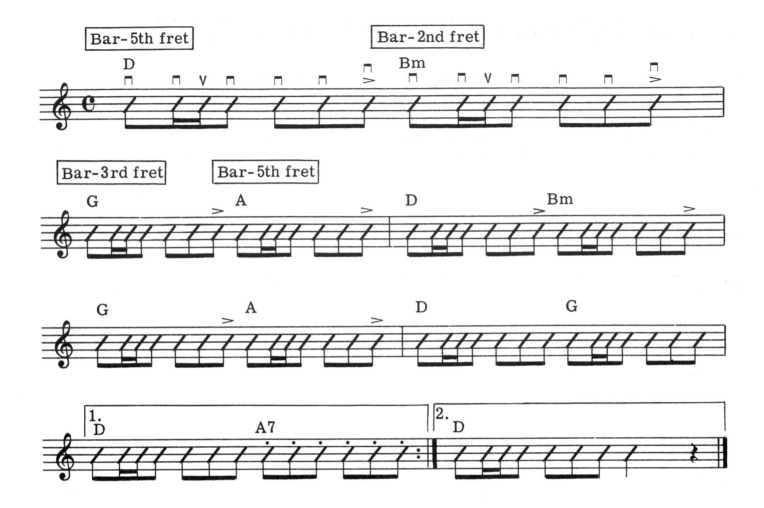

Try this rhythm with some of the other turn-arounds you know.

We now come to the end of *PART II*. You know the major bar chords, the minor bar chords, and the 7th bar chords, in all positions. You know the standard blues progression (with variations) and the turn-around chord progression. And you know the most popular rock rhythms. In short, you know the chords, progressions, and rhythms used in most rock songs—about as much as most other rock 'n roll rhythm guitarists.

Along about this point in the book you should start playing in a rock 'n roll group. If you can't find a rock group to join, form your own. Check the bulletin board at your school or the local newspaper or with your friends and find a rock group that needs a rhythm guitarist and join up. The only way to become a good rhythm guitarist is to play rhythm guitar in a group.* And, of course, you should never miss the chance to see and hear other rock groups. Watch the rhythm guitarist and try to figure out exactly what he's doing. To sum up: start playing in a rock group; start listening to as much live rock music as you can; and start watching live rhythm guitarists do their thing.

PART III
ADVANCED RHYTHM GUITAR PLAYING

There are only two basic differences between the amateur rock guitarist and the professional. The professional listens more and thinks more. If you don't listen to a song when you play it, the song will never get off the ground. Listen and think of interesting things to do to make the song more dynamic. In this next section I will show you some of the things professionals do in certain situations. After that, you're on your own.

6th Chords

The 6th chord is an important rock 'n roll chord. To learn it first make an F chord behind the 1st fret.

F chord

Now reposition the 4th finger on the 2nd string for an F6 chord:

F6 chord

Make the 3rd finger bend slightly so that it touches the 4th string and blocks the sound from that string.

Strum this chord at a few different frets until you're sure you know it. This 6th chord has the same letter name as the *root 6 bar chord*, and you locate it the same way.

The use of the major chord, the 6th chord, and the 7th chord with the same bar position is very popular. Here is that combination including chord diagrams so you can see how simple this progression is to play. Block the sound from the 4th string during this progression.

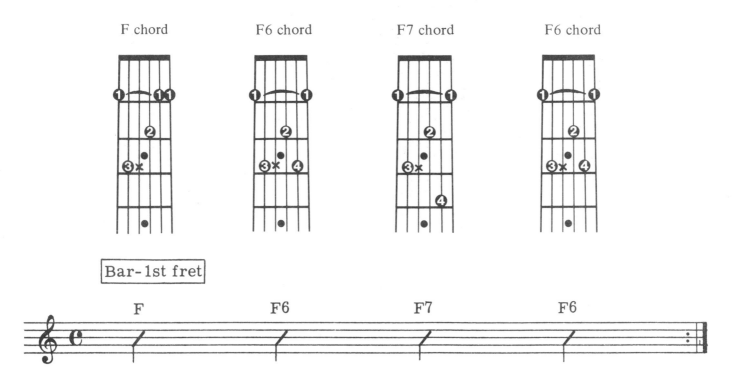

Play this progression a few times and listen carefully to the 2nd string. The rock sound of this progression comes from the movement of this string.

To change the major *root 5 bar chord* to a 6th chord is quite simple: just allow the 3rd finger to include the 1st string in the small bar.

Bb6 chord

This 6th chord has the same letter name as the *root 5 bar chord*, and you locate it the same way. Starting with the *root 5 bar chord*, here's a typical progression using this 6th chord. Pay particular attention to the sound of the 1st string as you play.

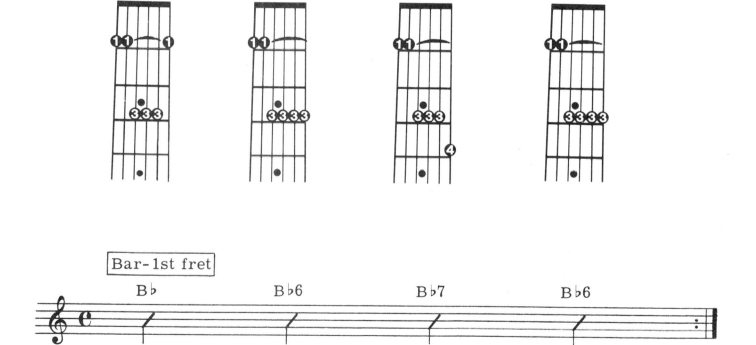

Put these two patterns together for a really swinging and, I hope, familiar rendition of the blues. Notice that you use only down-strokes of the pick with accented staccato chords on the "&" of each beat. This manner of strumming makes for a driving rhythm.

Blues in F

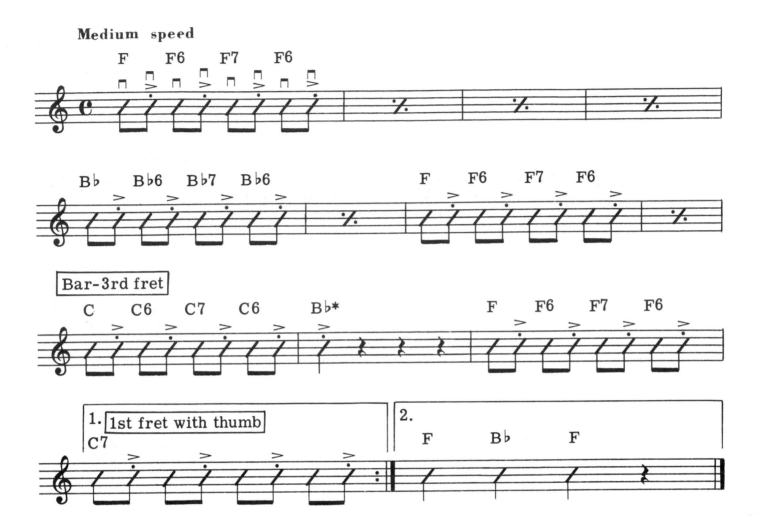

Another typical rhythm for this progression is the modified triplet rhythm known as the "shuffle." To get the shuffle rhythm simply avoid playing on the "2" of the triplet rhythm. As before, use only down-strokes of the pick.

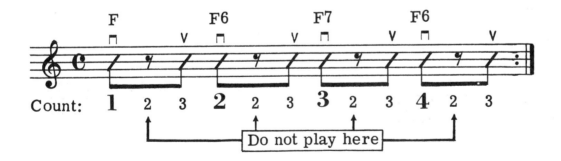

The eighth note rest (𝄾) in the triplet figure (⌐⌐𝄾⌐) indicates the shuffle rhythm. Practice the example until it feels comfortable to you. Now go back and do the previous blues (in F) using the shuffle rhythm.

To make the shuffle rhythm more dynamic play a staccato strum on the beat. Notice the open-string chord at the end of each measure is played with a pick up-stroke.

The lead guitarist fills in here for the last three beats.

Blues in A

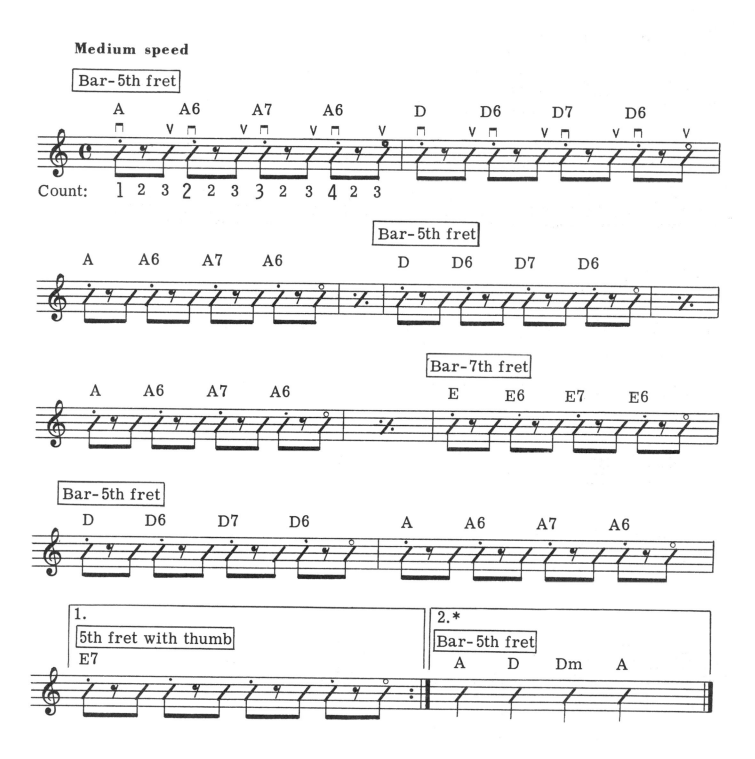

A very interesting and useful variation of this progression follows. Here the essence of the progression is transferred to the bass strings. Try this playing only the fingered strings.

*This type of ending is known as the "church" or "amen" ending. It can be used as the ending to any kind of song.

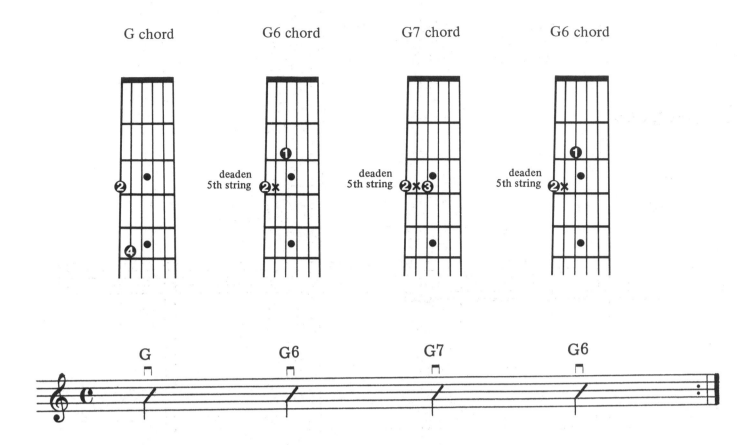

Notice that you play only the bass strings. With the G6 and G7 chords,
deaden the 5th string with the 2nd finger. The 2nd finger's position on the
6th string gives you the letter name of the progression. Repeat the fingering
one string away from you for the next chord in the blues.

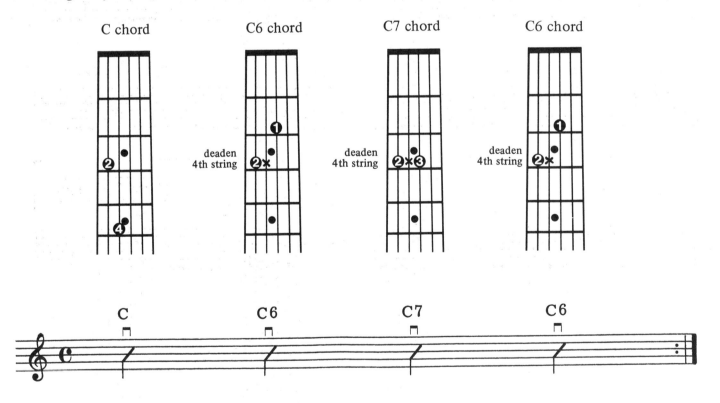

As before play only the fingered strings. The 2nd finger gives you the letter
name and also deadens the 4th string.

Now try the blues progression with these variations. Use the shuffle rhythm and only down-strokes of the pick. Played in this manner at a slow speed, the blues takes on a rather unhappy kind of feeling.

Blues in G

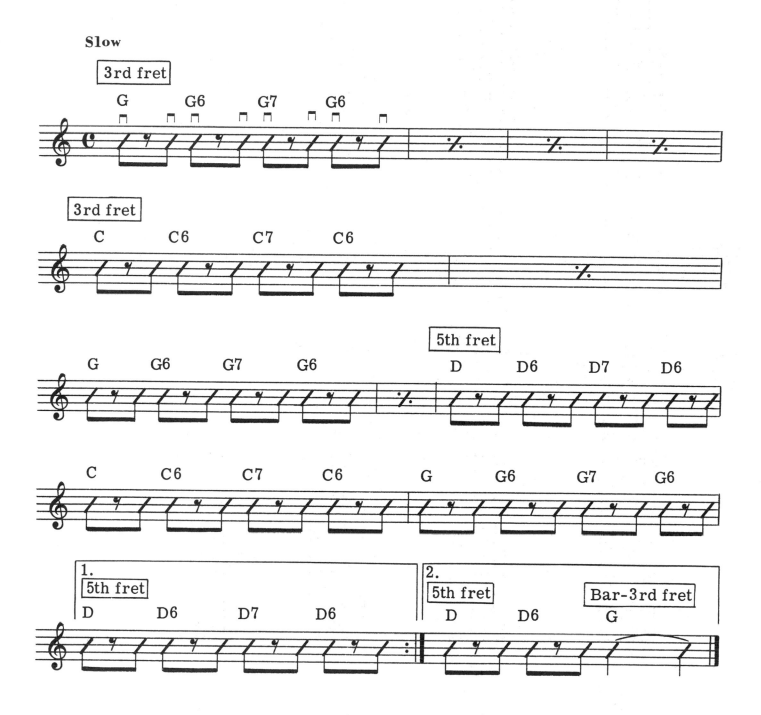

Arpeggios

One of the favorite techniques of professional rhythm guitarists is to play chords in single notes rather than strums. If you'll recall from *Minor Chords* (page 52) when you see a wedge-mark with a number under it you play only the string indicated by the number. In the example below, finger the open C chord but play only the 5th string.

Following the string indications below the wedge-marks, try this example. Carefully follow the pick directions: three down-strokes followed by three up-strokes. The rhythm is in triplets.

This should sound quite nice if you're doing it right. On the 1st beat after you position the pick on the 3rd string, let it glide over the 3rd and 2nd strings with the same downward motion of the pick. On the 2nd beat use one upward motion of the pick.

Play the turn around in C using this new technique. Notice that the top three strings are consistently used in this method of playing chords (properly called an "arpeggio" because the effect is similar to that of a harp). Play it quite slow.

Turn Around in C

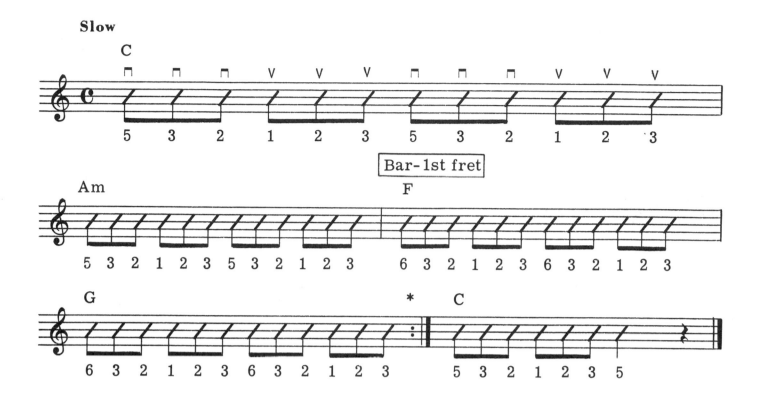

Slow progressions such as the turn around are often concluded with what's known as a major 7th chord. One of the easier major 7th chord formations is derived from the *root 5 bar chord*.

Bb Major 7 chord

Strum this Bb Major 7 chord a few times listening for the very particular quality of the major 7th chord. The letter name of this new chord is the same as the *root 5 bar chord*. When this chord is at the 1st fret you have a Bb Major 7 chord, at the 3rd fret a C Major 7 chord, at the 5th fret a D Major 7 chord, etc.

*When you come to this repeat sign, you repeat the whole progression. The second time you come to it you just keep on going to the end.

Play this turn around in D using arpeggios, bar chords, and our new major
7th chord.

Turn Around in D

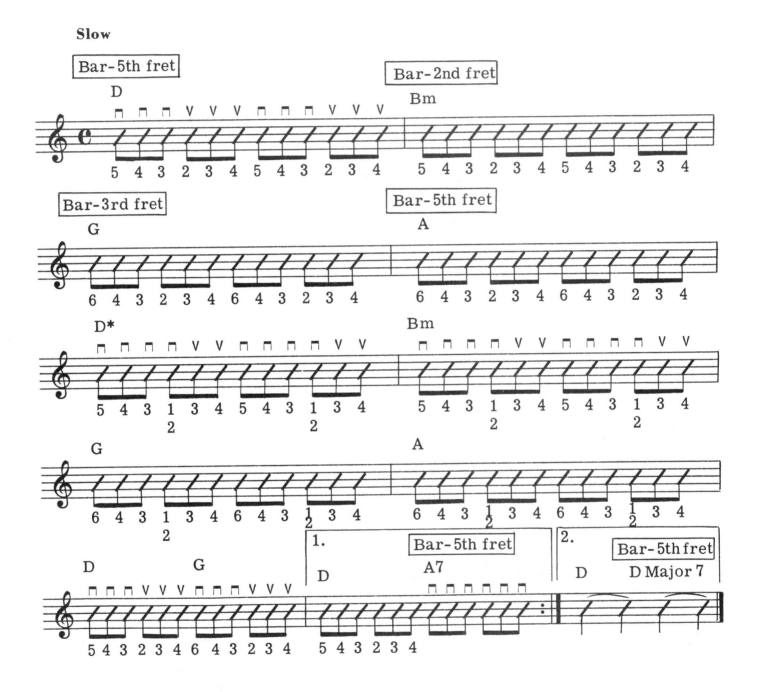

*Beginning with this chord there is a slight variation in the pattern. Play both the 2nd
and 1st strings together with a down-stroke on beats 2 and 4.

Here's another very useful major 7th chord.

G Major 7 chord

The 1st finger blocks the sound from the 5th string.

Notice that the index finger frets not only the 6th string but the 1st string as well. Strum the chord at a few different frets trying for a clear sound. Deaden the sound from the 1st string if you can't get it to sound right.

Both the root and letter name of this new chord are on the 6th string. When the chord is behind the 3rd fret you have a G Major 7 chord, behind the 5th fret an A Major 7 chord, behind the 7th fret a B Major 7 chord, etc. Play this short turn around ending with this new major 7th chord.

Turn Around in A

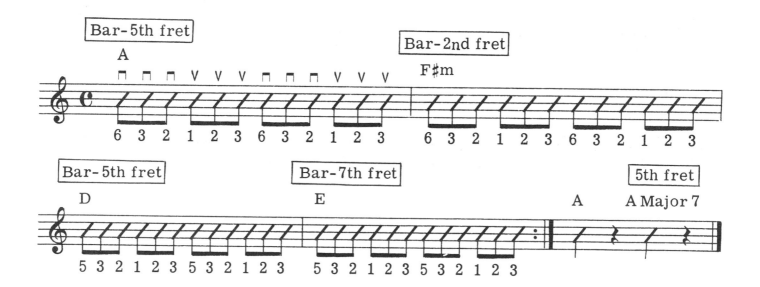

Connecting Chords

One of the more beautiful things a rhythm guitarist can do is to connect the chords in a progression by using bass-note runs. To better understand how to play single notes that are not a part of an arpeggio, play the following song. The second number beneath the wedge-mark stands for the fret you use to produce the note.

For example, the first note is produced by playing the 6th string open and the second note by playing the 6th string at the 4th fret. A third number tells which left hand finger to use. Play it at a very slow speed at first without rushing. You'll like this one.

Guitar Boogie

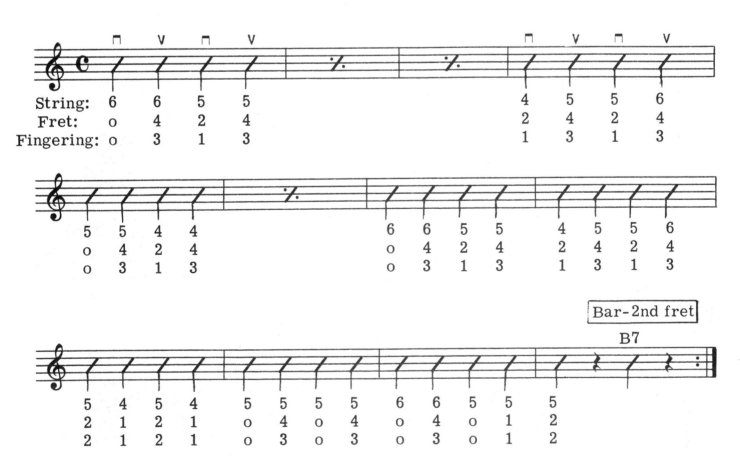

For a variation, do the song again playing two notes to each beat.

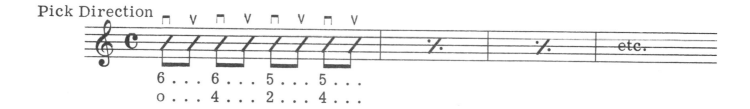

6 . . . 6 . . . 5 . . . 5 . . .
o . . . 4 . . . 2 . . . 4 . . .

The shuffle rhythm also sounds nice.

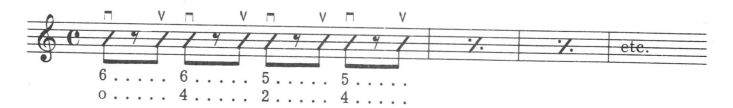

6 . . . . . 6 . . . . . 5 . . . . . 5 . . . . .
o . . . . . 4 . . . . . 2 . . . . . 4 . . . . .

By combining single string playing with the regular chord strums, you end up with a very professional sound. The more familiar of these combinations occur in slow moving chord progressions such as the turn-around. The next turn-around shows two different ways to connect the chords in this progression. Practice it until it sounds smooth and pretty.

Turn Around in C

*The left hand fingerings and the fret numbers are the same: to finger the 3rd fret use the 3rd finger, the 2nd fret the 2nd finger.

In the next turn around, play the chords in single notes (arpeggios) with connecting bass-note runs. This is a very satisfying way to accompany songs on the slow and dreamy side. Bring out the bass-note runs by accenting them slightly. As in the previous turn around, the left hand fingerings and the fret numbers are the same in the connecting runs.

Turn Around in G

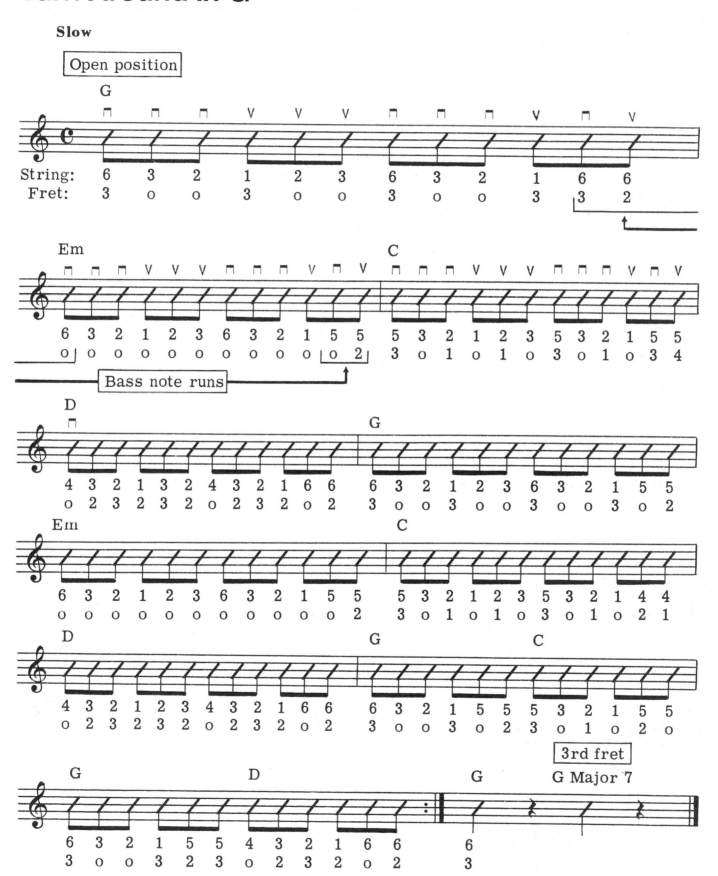

Play through the *Turn Around in F* (page 56) using open chords and come up with bass-note runs similar to the ones used in the C and G turn arounds. Before we move away from the turn arounds forever and ever, play this bar position turn around. Because it is played using bar chords, you'll be able to play this most sophisticated version of the turn around in almost any key.

Turn Around in A

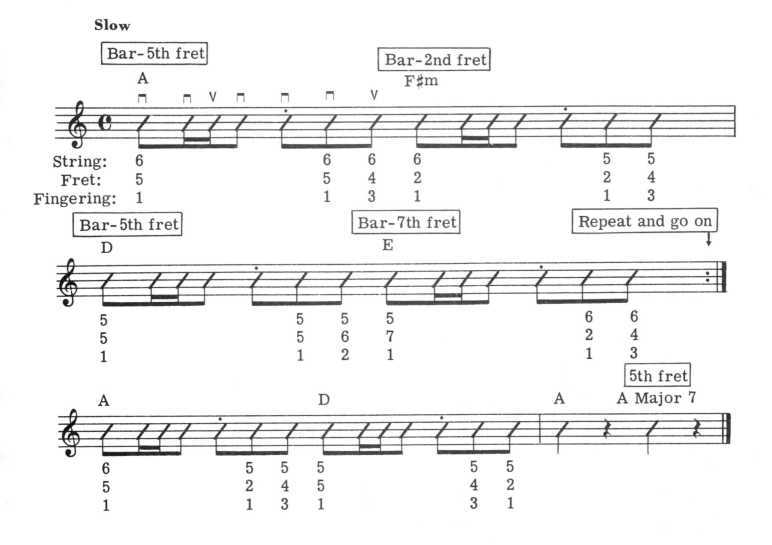

Some New Things

On to new and exciting chord connecting bass-note runs. These type of runs add much to the drive of fast moving songs. In the next progression, notice that some of the notes in the runs are to be played staccato. Use the same technique for playing staccato notes as you did with staccato chords. The ties you remember from *ROCK PROGRESSIONS #2* (page 48). Play it through a few times on the slow side and then speed it up. Play the accented chords with a good and strong down-stroke of the pick.

Blues in Bb

Fast

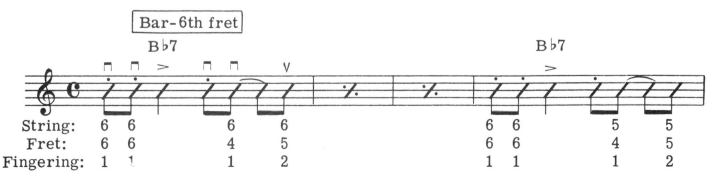

| Bar-6th fret | | | | | |
| Bb7 | | | | | Bb7 |

String:	6	6	6	6	6	6	5	5
Fret:	6	6	4	5	6	6	4	5
Fingering:	1	1	1	2	1	1	1	2

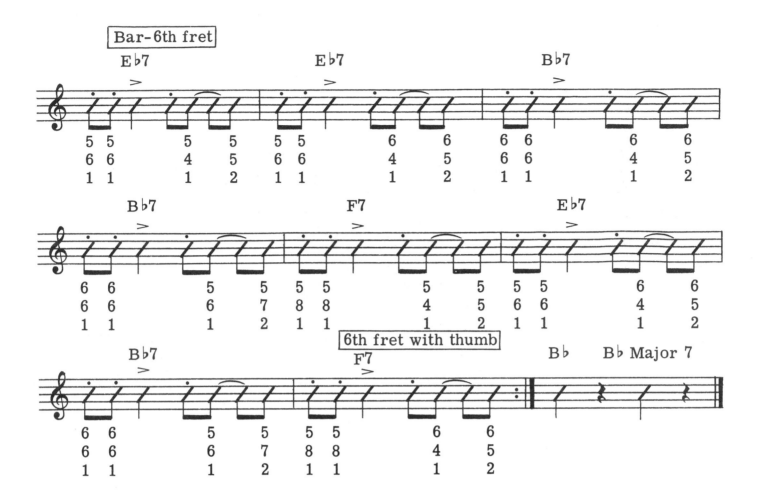

Examine the Bb progression again. Notice that once the bass-note run was established in the 1st measure, it remained essentially the same for the rest of the blues. With this type of run, once you learn the 1st measure you can play the entire blues.

We'll take up another progression after you learn a new way to play the open-string chord. First make the C chord with the bar behind the 3rd fret. Now pick up the 3rd finger of the left hand leaving only the bar. This bar by the 1st finger alone is called the open-bar chord or abbreviated by simply "OB." Here's how it works.

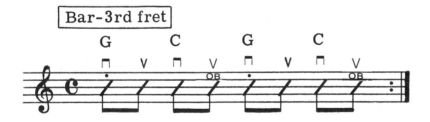

In the above example, the bar stays down for the entire measure. The open-bar chord is used in place of the open-string chord. Here's a blues progression using the new open-bar chord with a somewhat different bass-note run. Songs are played and recorded with bass-note runs exactly like those used in these progressions so do your homework well. Because this progression uses bar chords, you can (and should) play it in other keys. This one uses the shuffle rhythm.

Blues in G

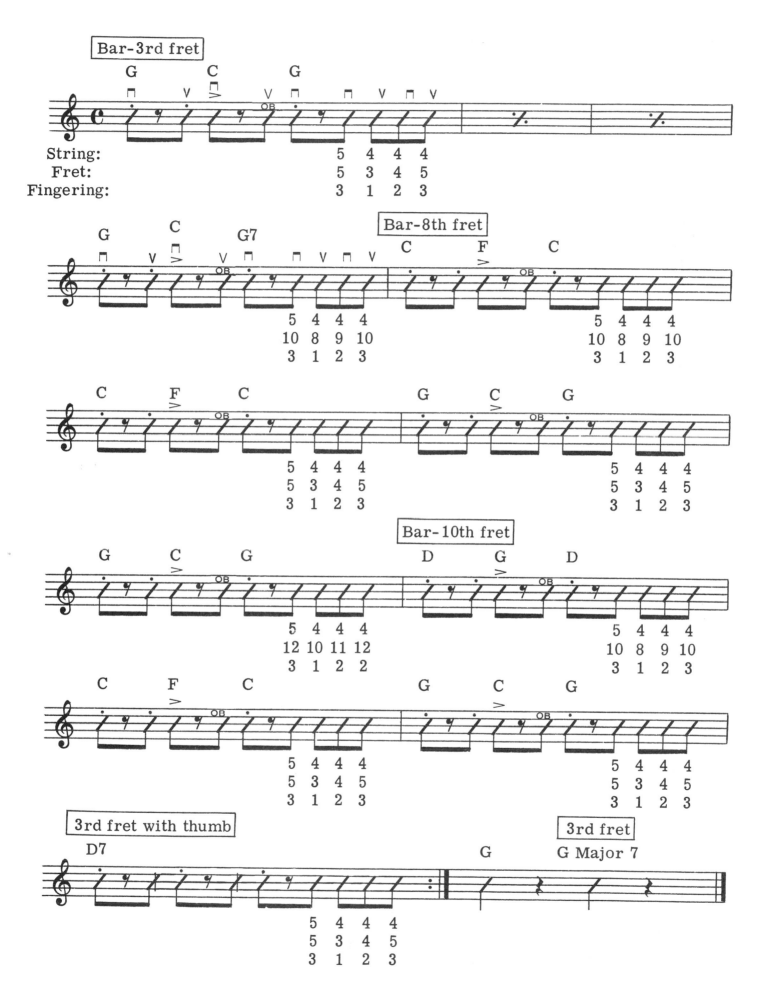

Often the rhythm guitar bass-note runs are the best remembered part of a song. Here's a rhythm chart in the style of *In The Midnight Hour.** Truly the right rhythm with the right bass-note run can make a good song great.

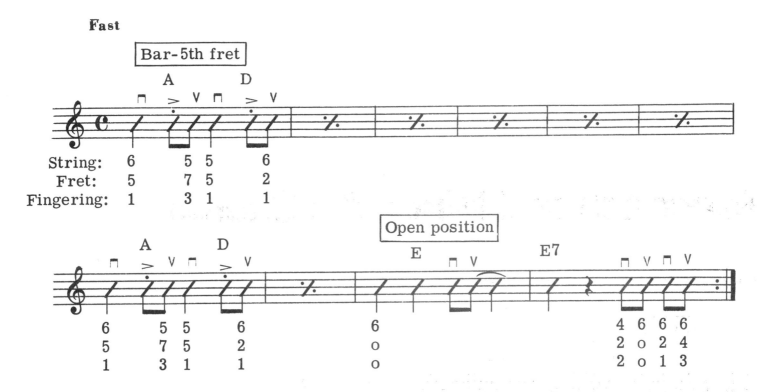

You must have heard hundreds of bass-note runs similar to the ones used in this lesson. The thing to do now is to start playing a blues progression (in A, for example) using one of the bass-note runs that we've covered. When you come to the repeat sign, vary the bass-note run and play through the progression again. Keep repeating the progression over and over using any runs that sound good to you. Let your imagination and your listening experience be your guide.

*See *The Best of Wilson Picket* (Atlantic 8151).

Minor 6th and Minor 7th Chords

Play this familiar rock progression using 6th and 7th chords.

To convert this entire progression to the minor, simply raise the 2nd finger.
Here are the chord diagrams:

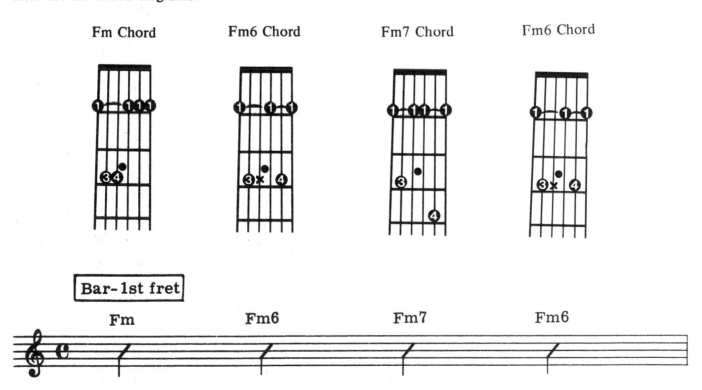

Play this progression in the minor a few times and then play it in the major
(the way you've been playing it) and listen to the difference. Played in the
minor the progression has a very soft, jazz like feeling.

The minor 6th (m6) and the minor 7th (m7) chords used here are both *root 6 bar chords*. When you want to finger one of these two chords first make the minor chord of the same letter name, and then add the pinky turning the minor chord into a minor 6th or 7th chord.

Starting with the other minor chord you know, here's an alternate way of playing the same progression.

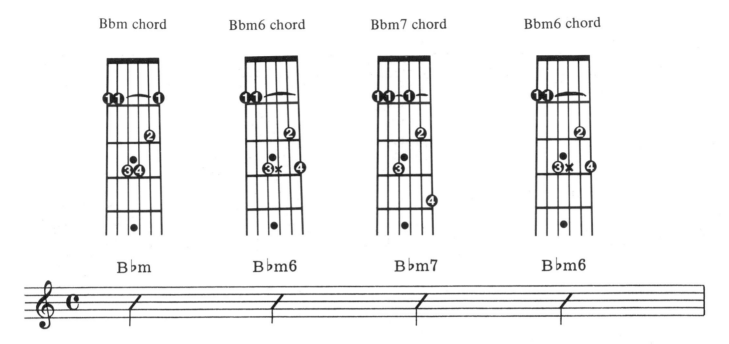

Both of these minor 6th and 7th chords are *root 5 bar chords*. It's quite easy to finger these two chords if you'll make the minor *root 5 bar chord* first and then simply add the pinky.

We'll take up a rock progression with these new chords in it as soon as you learn this rhythm variation. Start by playing the F chord in the triplet rhythm and counting.

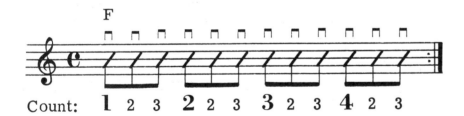

Keep counting the same rhythm but don't play on the "3" of each triplet.

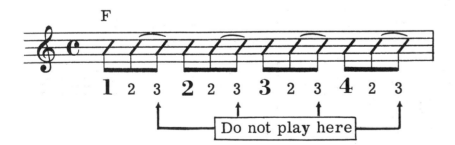

The tie between the "2" and the "3" indicates this rhythm. It has a sort of limping feeling and is frequently used with other rhythms. On to the new rock progression. Watch out for the staccato strums!

84

New Rock Progression

The minor 6th and minor 7th chords also work quite well in jazz progressions. We'll take this up in the next lesson.

9th Chords

Still another new and wonderful chord to learn is the 9th chord. To learn one first make the F7 chord at the 1st fret.

F7 chord

Simply move the pinky away from you one string to make an F9 chord.

F9 chord

After you're sure you have the chord fingered right, strum it a few times and listen for the very particular quality of the 9th chord. The sound of the 1st string gives the chord its flavor. This 9th chord is a *root 6 bar chord* so locating it should be no problem. With the bar at the 3rd fret you have a G9 chord, at the 5th fret an A9 chord, at the 7th fret a B9 chord, etc. We'll go straight into a progression using 9th chords as soon as you learn one more.

The other important 9th chord has its root on the 5th string. This is a very unusual chord to finger. Bar the top three strings with the 3rd finger and deaden the 6th string with the thumb. Try it.

B9 chord

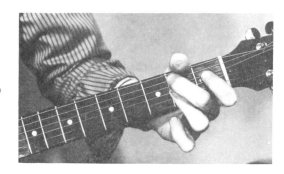

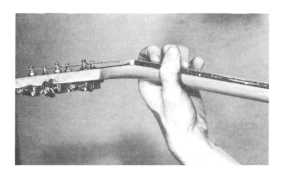

Work on this chord for awhile until it sounds good. Since this chord has its root on the 5th string, the position of the 2nd finger will give you the letter name of the chord. At the 2nd fret you have a B9 chord, at the 3rd fret a C9 chord, at the 5th fret a D9 chord, etc. Got that? Good! On to a progression that uses all the new chords presented in this and the last lesson.

One of the prettiest and most melodic of all progressions is blues in the jazz style. Set the tone control on your guitar for maximum bass, and play this blues with light and graceful strums.

Jazz Blues in Bb

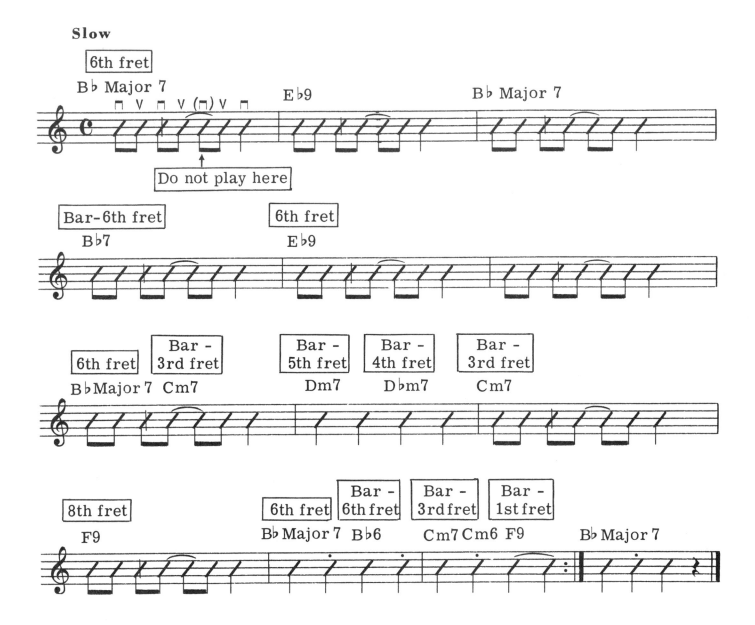

This type of jazz feeling often adds to the interest of slow songs. By substituting major 7th chords for major chords, minor 7th chords for minor chords, and 9th chords for 7th chords, almost any slow song will take on a jazz flavor. Follow this formula:

1) Play major 7th chords in place of major chords,
2) minor 7th chords in place of minor chords,
3) and 9th chords in place of 7th chords.

Here's the familiar turn around with a jazz flavor.

Turn Around in Bb

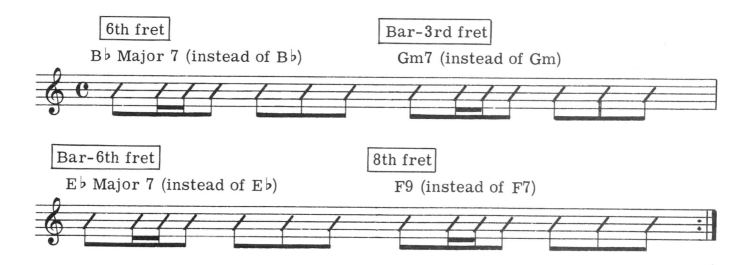

The 9th chord is also frequently used in the standard rock progression.
We'll take up that use as soon as you learn this very useful rhythm. Bar the
A chord at the 5th fret and try this rhythm:

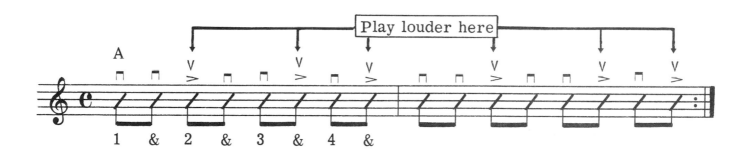

Make sure you're bringing out the accents good and strong. For a better
sound, play only the three bass strings on the unaccented strums. This will
make the accented strums stand out even more. Now speed it up. This is
a very important rock rhythm so don't be afraid to spend some time with it.

Here's a blues to play using our new rhythm and also using 9th chords. A
favorite way to begin playing a blues is to start at the 9th measure. This
gives the singer a feeling for the rhythm and the key before he starts singing at measure 1. Play this blues a few times and you'll understand what
I mean.

Blues in A

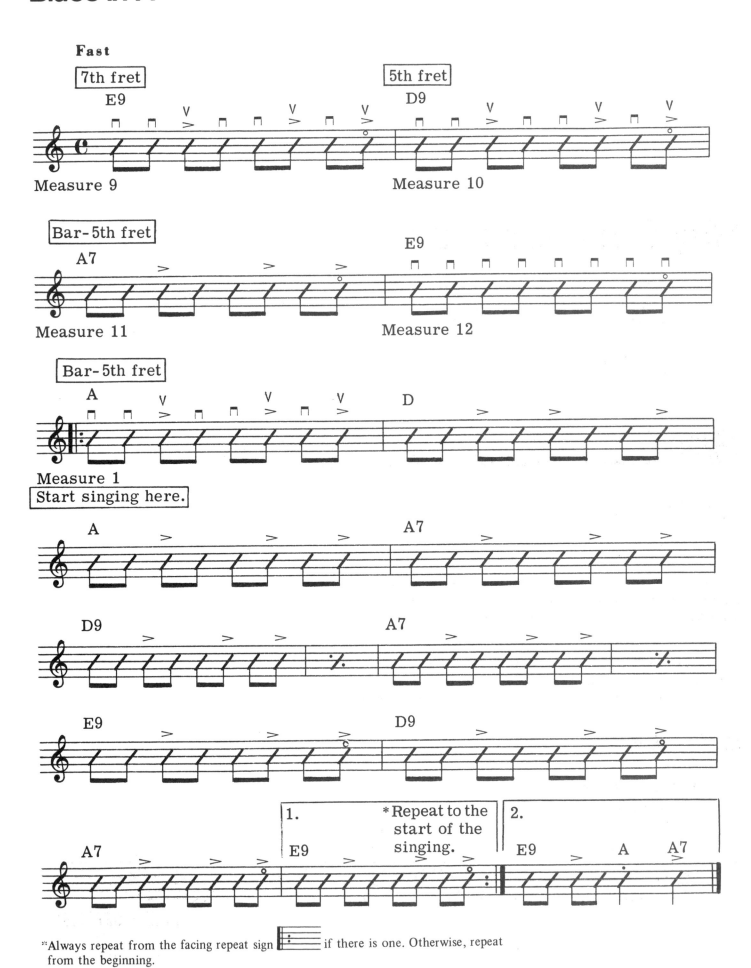

"Always repeat from the facing repeat sign 𝄆═══ if there is one. Otherwise, repeat from the beginning.

Rhythm Exercises

About the quickest way to improve your rhythm guitar playing is by practicing rhythm exercises. One of the more popular exercises uses a familiar chord pattern played in triplets. Try this example.

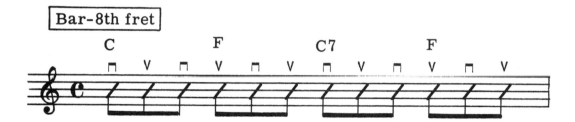

Notice that the pick direction changes with each strum. Now play the example again but this time watch the thumb of the left hand. The thumb and the bar should remain in the same position while you're changing chords.

Before we take up this exercise, let me ask you a question: Did you ever get the metronome that we talked about earlier? These exercises are designed around a metronome so if you can borrow or buy one, please do so. If you can't get hold of one, don't worry about it—you'll still benefit from the exercise.

Set the metronome at 60 (one beat or "tick" a second) and get ready to start playing. Notice that the chord patterns in each measure are the same as the 1st measure except they're at a lower fret. Here we go.

Exercise

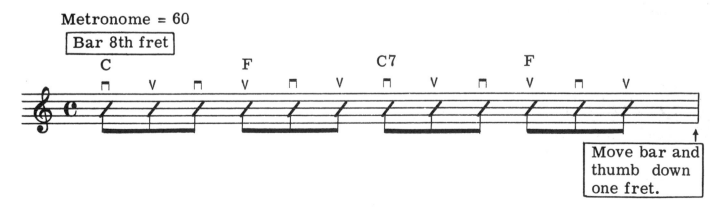

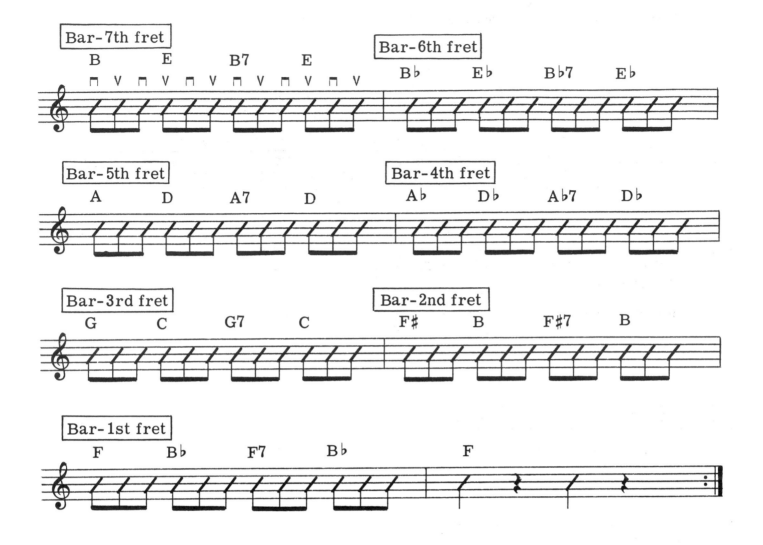

If your left hand gets very tired and starts to ache with pain, pause for a minute or so and then continue the exercise. Try to keep the movement of the right hand as quiet as possible, moving the hand from the wrist when you strum. Leave the metronome set at 60 today and play the exercise about five minutes. The next time you practice, play the exercise with the metronome set at 63 (slightly faster). In this manner, day by day, gradually increase the speed of the exercise until the metronome setting is around 160. This should take at least three weeks. The thing to remember is make sure you're comfortable playing the exercise at a given speed before you try to play it faster. You might even keep a little chart like so to help you remember.

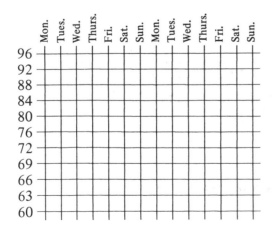

A second way to play the same exercise is to start with a pick up-stroke.

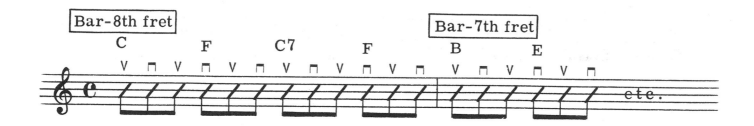

Continue this variation through the entire exercise. Accompany the first exercise (starting with a pick down-stroke) with this version (starting with an up-stroke) in your daily practice.

For the next exercise you'll have to learn a new time value. Let's review the old ones first. When you see one wedge-mark on a beat, you strum one time:

By inserting "&" between each number, you play twice on each beat. The two wedge-marks are connected by a bar.

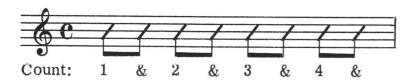

Divide the beat into four equal parts by inserting "a." Instead of counting "1 & 2 &," count "1–a–&–a 2–a–&–a." This will be clearer to you after you play this example. Follow the pick directions carefully.

This new rhythm is indicated by *two bars* connecting the wedge-marks. This gives you a third way to practice the same exercise.

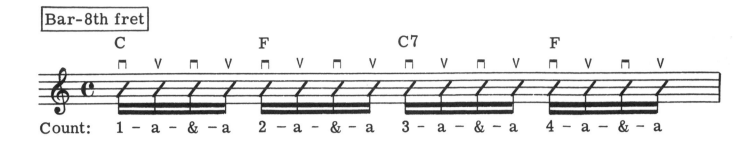

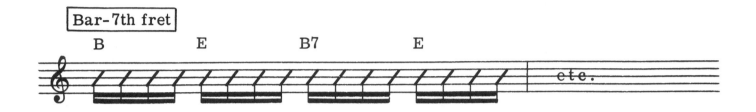

A variation of this exercise produces the "train" rhythm. This rhythm is quite popular with soul guitarists so spend some time with it. Play the top three strings on the "1-a-" of each beat and the bottom two strings on the "&-a." The sound of this rhythm is similar to that of a locomotive which accounts for its name. Try it:

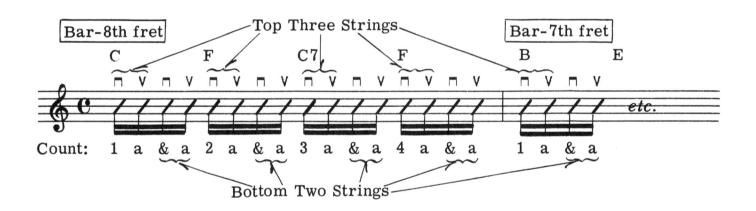

Please remember that the object of these exercises is not to see how fast you can play them, but how smooth and relaxed and controlled you can play them.* Remember to increase the speed gradually, day by day, on all three exercises. Practicing this type of exercise will make a good rhythm guitarist great.

*Playing one or more of the exercises presented in this lesson right before your band is going to perform is an excellent way to "warm up." When you're using an exercise to warm up, don't play for more than a few minutes as your left hand gets too tired to play well.

New Chords

In this lesson we'll take up the remaining few chords that are used by professional rock guitarists. First of all, let me introduce to you a new way to form a 7th chord.

Eb7 chord

Strum the chord a few times being careful not to strum the 6th string. Like the other bar chords, this is a movable chord. With its root on the 4th string, this chord is a *root 4 bar chord*.

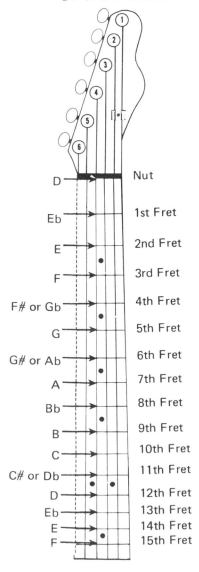

NOTES PRODUCED BY THE 4TH STRING

D	Nut
Eb	1st Fret
E	2nd Fret
F	3rd Fret
F# or Gb	4th Fret
G	5th Fret
G# or Ab	6th Fret
A	7th Fret
Bb	8th Fret
B	9th Fret
C	10th Fret
C# or Db	11th Fret
D	12th Fret
Eb	13th Fret
E	14th Fret
F	15th Fret

In the illustration on the right, the letters stands for the notes of the 4th string. Familiarize yourself ·with them.

To locate a *root 4 bar chord* first find the letter-name of the chord on the 4th string and then make the bar behind that fret. For example, for an Eb7 chord you bar behind the 1st fret, for an E7 chord bar at the 2nd fret, for an F7 chord bar at the 3rd fret, etc.

Let's get back to our new 7th chord. By using this 7th chord with the *root 6* 7th chord, you create a more exciting rhythmic background (that's what you're supposed to be doing). By playing the same chord at different frets you create a feeling of motion within the chord. Here's a rock progression to show you what I mean. Use the 1st finger of the left hand to finger the bass-note runs.

96

Rock Progression

Fast

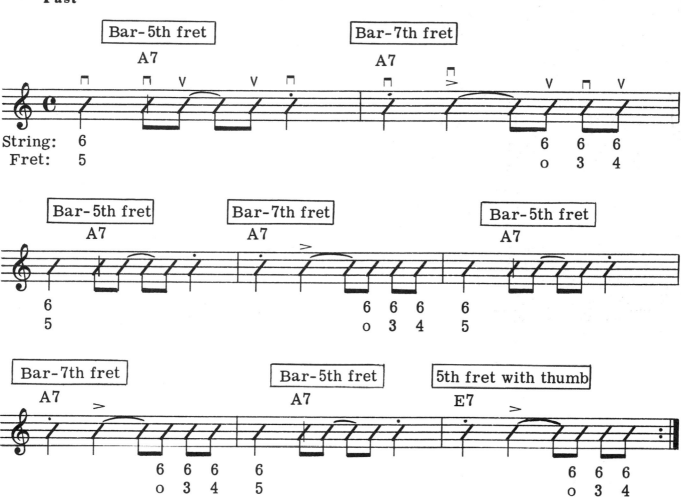

And the *root 4 bar chord* has its own minor chord formation. Finger and play this Eb minor chord a few times.

Ebm chord

As with the 7th chord, the position the bar takes on the 4th string determines the letter name of this chord. Behind the 2nd fret you have an E minor chord, behind the 3rd fret an F minor chord, etc. The following turn around illustrates one way you can use this new minor chord. The second time through the progression use the *root 6 bar chord* for the F# minor chord and mentally compare it to the sound of the *root 4 bar chord*.

Turn Around in A

Slow

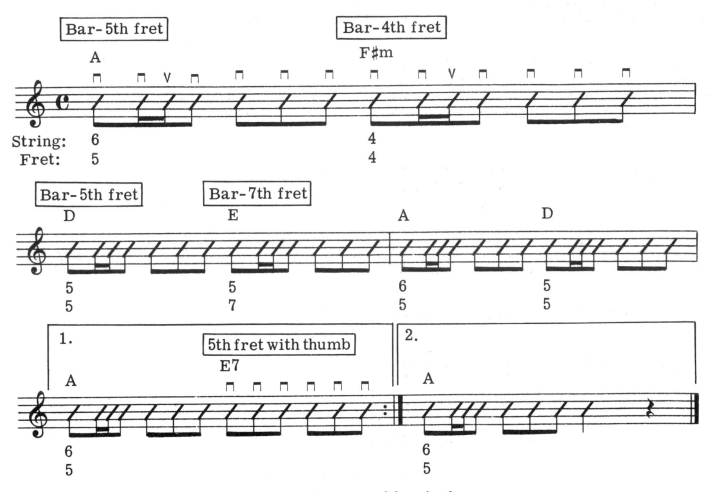

Bar-5th fret		Bar-4th fret
A		F#m

String: 6 / 4
Fret: 5 / 4

Bar-5th fret	Bar-7th fret		
D	E	A	D

5 / 5 / 6 / 5
5 / 7 / 5 / 5

1.
A — 5th fret with thumb — E7

6
5

2.
A

6
5

If you're playing a very slow song using arpeggios, you might mix the *root 6 bar chord* and the *root 4 bar chord* together like so to create an interesting background.

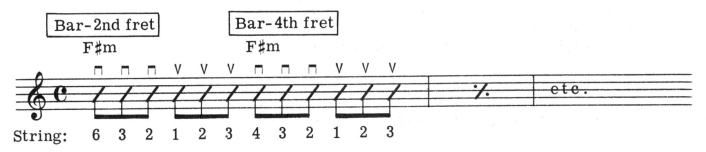

Bar-2nd fret	Bar-4th fret
F#m	F#m

String: 6 3 2 1 2 3 4 3 2 1 2 3   */.*   etc.

A very important chord that we haven't covered yet is the *augmented chord*. It is generally abbreviated *aug* or *+*. Finger and play this F augmented chord:

F aug chord

Be especially careful not to strum the 5th and 6th strings when you play this chord. The root of the chord is on the 4th string so the position of the 4th finger on that string gives you its letter-name. For example, when the 4th finger is behind the 3rd fret of the 4th string, you have an F aug. chord; behind the 5th fret you have a G aug. chord, etc. Practice this chord by playing it at a few different frets and naming, out loud, the chord as you play it.

You usually find this chord (and you don't find it used very often) in introductions to songs. If you have say a C minor chord as the first chord in a song, you might make a little introduction by inserting the augmented chord as in the following example. Leave the bar down at the 3rd fret while you play both chords.

With a *root 6 bar chord* you might play an introduction like this:

Although the augmented chord sounds sort of weird and interesting, don't over-use it.

An even rarer chord is the 7+5 chord. When a 7+5 chord is called for use an augmented chord of the same letter name. For example, if you see a C 7+5 chord notated in a song play a C augmented chord instead. For other rare chords like 7-9 or 7+9 or 11th chords, play a 7th chord of the same letter name. For example, for a C 7-9 or C 7+9 or C 11 chord play a C7 chord.

Another interesting chord is the *diminished chord*. This chord is generally abbreviated *dim.* or º. Finger and play the Eb diminished chord:

Eb dim chord

As with the augmented chord, you do not play the 5th and 6th strings when you strum the diminished chord. The root of this chord is on the 4th string so the position of the 1st finger on that string gives you the letter name. When the 1st finger is behind the 1st fret you have an Eb diminished chord, behind the 2nd fret you have an E diminished chord, behind the 3rd fret an F diminished chord, etc. Play this chord up and down the fingerboard naming the chord as you play it.

Play the following example to get an idea of how the diminished chord sounds when used in a song.

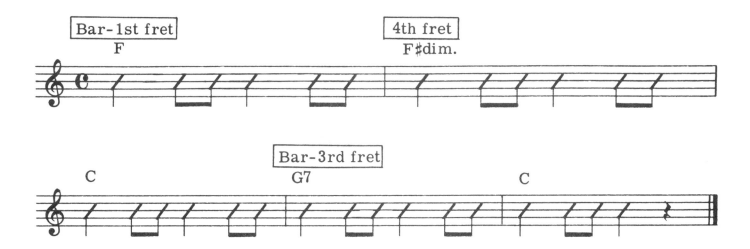

You now know all the chords used in rock 'n roll music! Not one chord will come up that you can't play.* You know all the basic rhythms and all the basic progressions! The rest of the book is going to be easy coasting.

*In case you forget how to play a chord, *APPENDIX* C is a complete list of all the chords used in rock 'n roll.

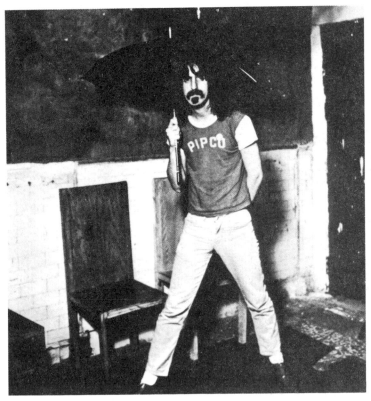

The English Sound

Up to this point we've been concentrating on the standard rock progression with variations along with the turn around progression. These progressions are the foundation of rock 'n roll. Any list of the top rock songs of the day will always include songs derived from or based totally on these progressions. But there are other influences—the impact of the English rock groups in the early 60's has caused a considerable change in the rock scene.

The most important single change that the English groups introduced to the rock scene was the increased emphasis on the words of a song rather than the regularity of a chord progression. Indeed the basis of the English or so called "Liverpool" sound are unusual chord progressions, very lyrical melodies, and a much more complete feeling from forms that approach classical music. The basic rock rhythms, however, never change.

Here's an example that illustrates a typical English rock progression. Notice that although it is exactly 12 bars long like the standard rock progression, the choice of chords gives it a very different feeling. Use the 1st finger of the left hand to finger the bass-note runs.

New Progression

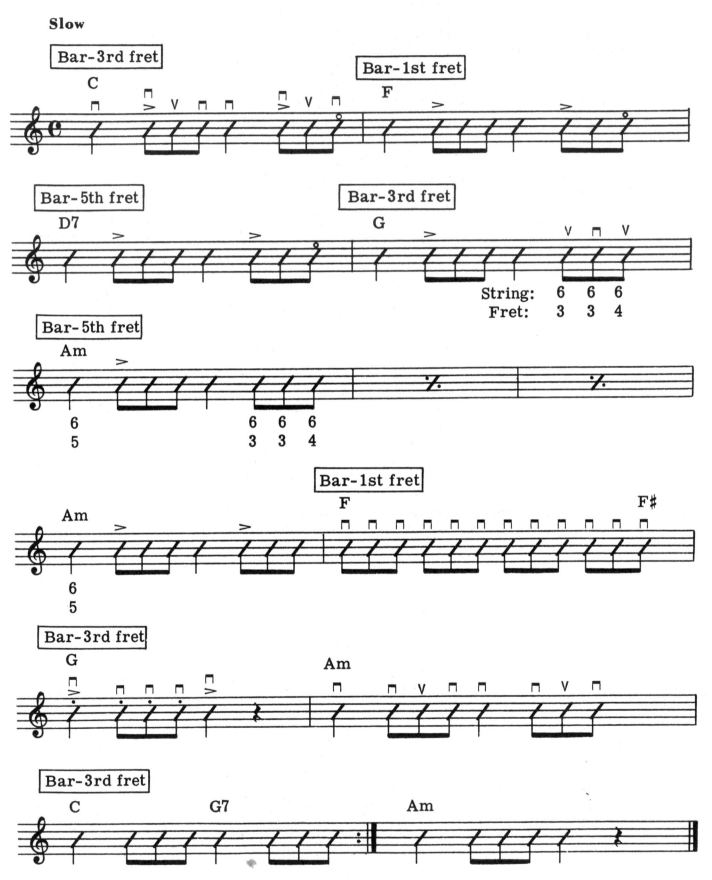

As the form of rock 'n roll songs became more complicated, you begin to find directional signs in the music traditionally associated with classical music. In the next progression (*New Progression #2*), notice that the 2nd ending is nine measures long! After the 2nd ending you'll see the directions *D. C. al fine.* This means you go back to the beginning of the song (*D. C.*) and play until you see the word *fine* (*al fine* means "to the end") at the 1st ending. That's where the song ends. The thing to remember is to immediately play the first measure without any pause or rhythmic break after you come to the directions *D. C. al fine.*

The rhythm is slightly different than anything you've played before so I'll give you an exercise to help you understand it. Play this four bar example counting as you play.

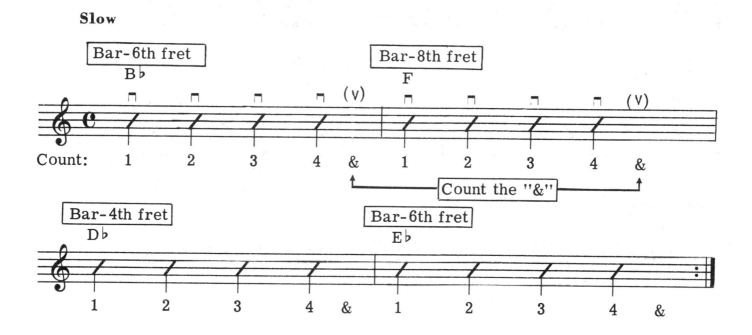

Now syncopate the beat by changing chords on the "&" instead of the "1." Play an accented up-stroke on the "&" and avoid strumming on the "1" except in the first measure.

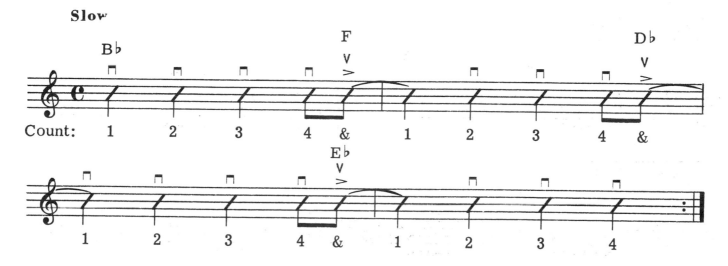

If you're playing this correctly, the feeling you should have at the "1" beat in each measure is sort of like skipping a step. If it doesn't you may have missed a step. Go back and check it over. If it sounds right then play this syncopated progression in the English style using directional signs (wow).

New Progression#2

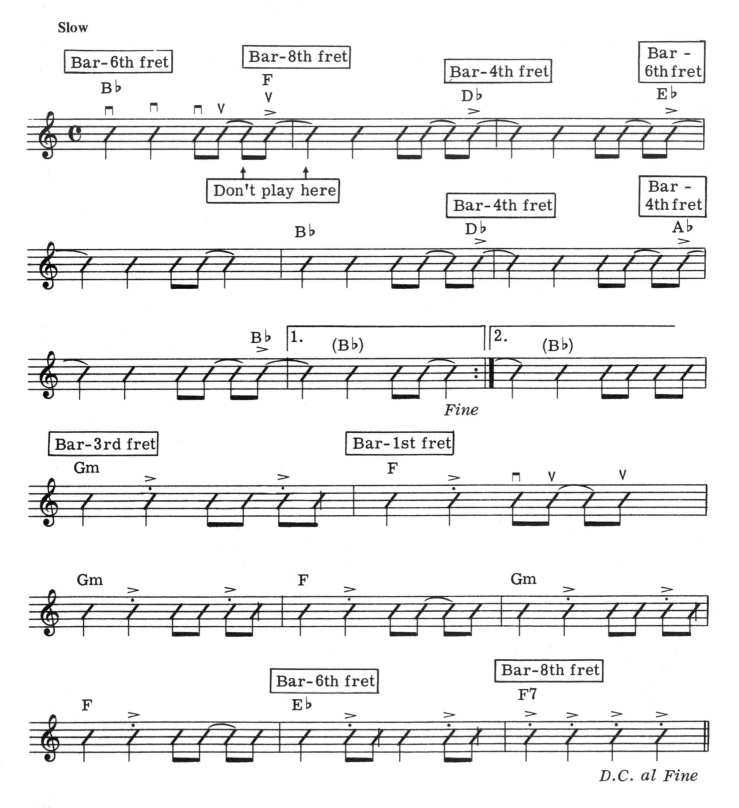

104

Folk Rock

In the mid 1960's another style of rock 'n roll emerged: folk rock. This style grew out of the increased awareness and popularity among city-dwellers of traditional American ballads and folksongs. Folk and country music bands generally consist of such instruments as unamplified guitars, banjos, fiddles, harmonicas, etc. By adding a strong rhythm section (drums, bass and rhythm guitars) with amplification, songs written in the folk style become folk rock.

By learning some of the rhythm guitar techniques from the folk rock bag, you add variety and interest to your playing. One of the more interesting and useful techniques in this style is a particular way of playing chords with single notes (arpeggios). Bar the G chord at the 3rd fret and play this example. Be careful to follow the pick directions, count, and play slowly (at first).

A Folk Style

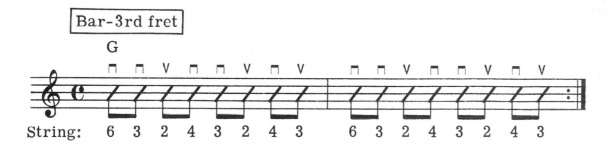

Practice this example for awhile until you're comfortable playing it. This style of playing chords is derived from folk guitarists who play with finger-picks rather than a flat pick. If you would like to try playing this style with your fingers instead of a pick, play the thumb on the 6th and 4th strings, the index finger on the 3rd string, and the middle finger on the 2nd string. Use the same rhythm as in the example. When you pluck a string, the finger should move toward the palm of the hand.

One thing you have to keep in mind when you play chords in this style is that the first note in the measure is the root of the chord. With a *root 6 bar chord*, as in the example, the first note is on the 6th string.

Try the standard rock progression in G using this method of playing chords. It'll sound very much like folk music although the progression is the standard rhythm 'n blues one. You'll have to play it pretty fast if it's going to sound like anything.

Blues in G

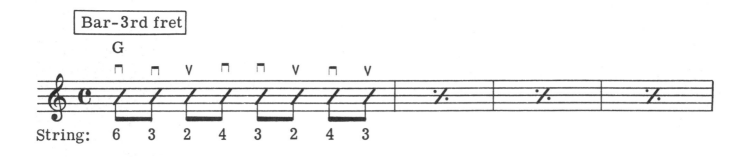

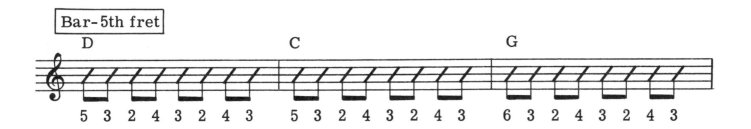

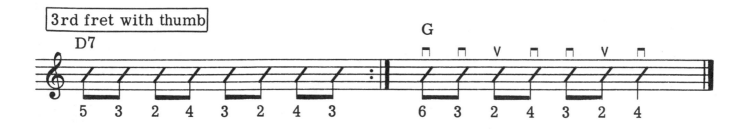

Present day rock groups often mix the folk style of playing chords with the regular way in order to get more contrast and interest in a song. Here's an example of this with still another new progression. Many slow songs, such as this one, sound better when you use open chords rather than bar chords. Keep this in mind when you're trying to figure out where to play the chords in a song.

Song

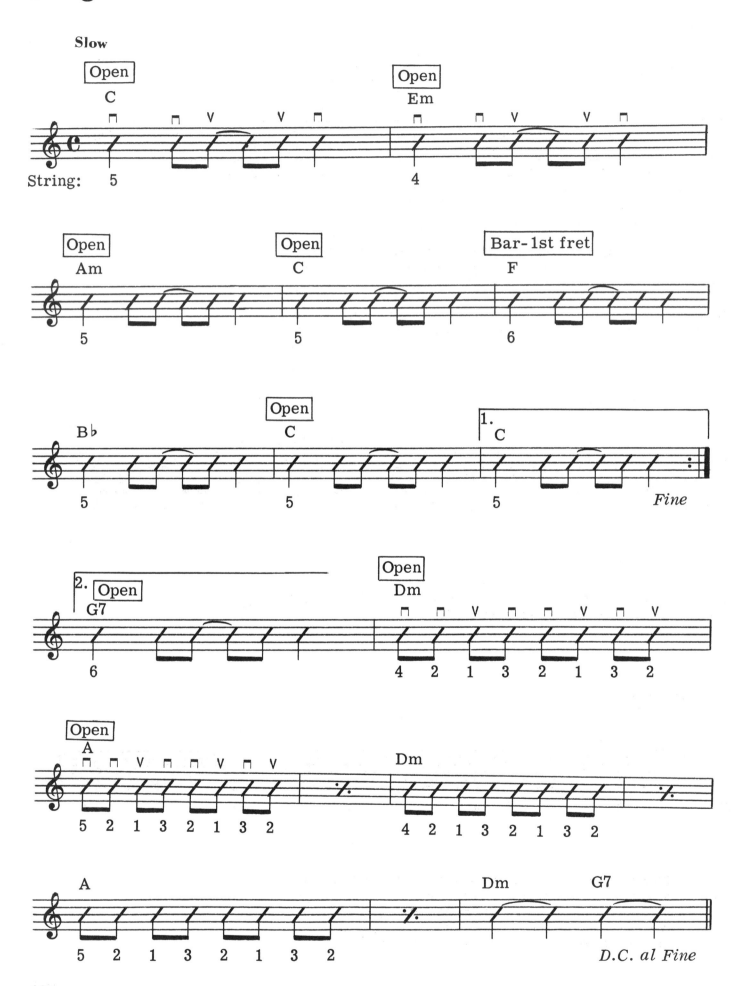

There's one other popular way of playing chords in this style. Play this example:

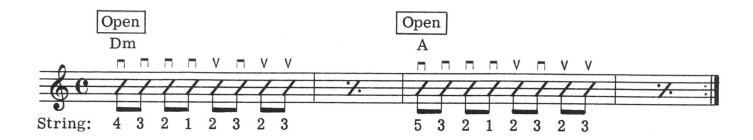

Played right, this style of playing chords creates a flowing sensation. After playing the example a few times, play the last progression again using this new style of playing chords for the D minor and A chords.

To learn another useful strum derived from folk music start playing and counting two strums on each beat. Use all down-strokes.

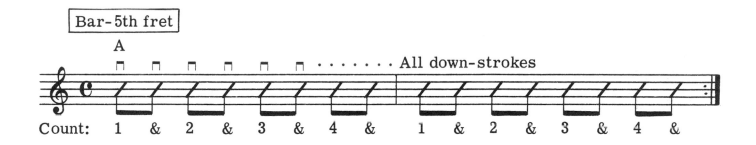

Keeping the same rhythm, insert an "a" after the "&": "1 &—a 2 &—a 3 &—a 4 &—a." Play an up-stroke on the "a."

Played right you can easily hear the division of the beat into two parts. Folk guitarists often count "BOM chuck-a BOM chuck-a . . ." in place of "1 &—a 2 &—a . . ." to better feel the rhythm. The next progression illustrates the use of this strum. The bass-note runs, which also have a folk flavor, are to be fingered with the 1st finger of the left hand.

A Folk Progression

Slow

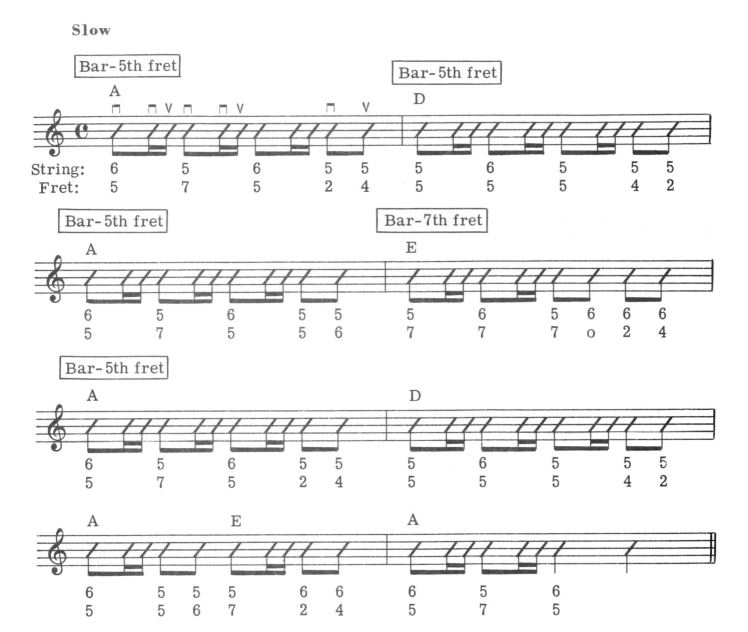

Advanced Rhythms

Here we go into learning some new and exciting rhythms! First, start playing the last folk strum we worked on.

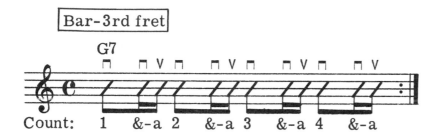

What we're going to do is tie the "&" to the previous wedge-mark. Keep the same rhythm going but don't play on the "&."

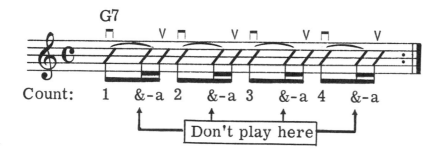

This is an important rhythm to work on. Try playing all down-strokes on the beat and right before you play the down-stroke, put a short up-stroke in. Count, "1 . . . a2 . . . a3 . . . a4 . . . a1 . . . a2 . . . etc." Played right, this rhythm has an angular feeling typical of today's so called "acid rock" sound. Here's a blues to work on using this new rhythm. Be sure to play the accents and staccato strums. The D7 chord in the 1st ending comes on the "&" instead of the "1" so be careful. Delaying the last chord a half-beat adds interest to a song and is a popular technique.

Blues in G

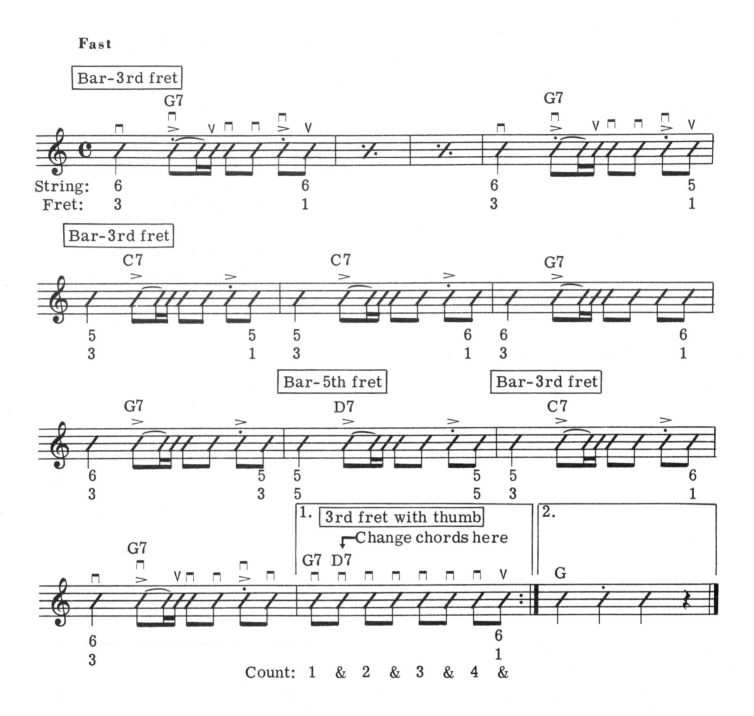

To learn another useful rhythm bar the A chord at the 5th fret and play this example using all down-strokes.

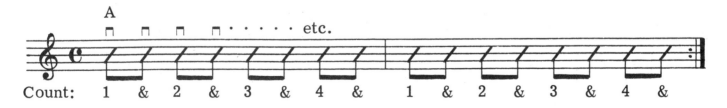

Keeping the same rhythm, insert an "a" before the "&": "1–a–& . . . 2–a
–& . . . 3–a–& . . . 4–a–& . . ." Play an up-stroke on the "a."

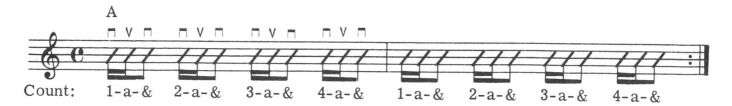

Count: 1-a-&   2-a-&   3-a-&   4-a-&   1-a-&   2-a-&   3-a-&   4-a-&

Played right you can still hear the division of the beat into two parts. Work
on this example for awhile until you're sure you have this new rhythm.

On to a rock progression using both the new rhythms in this lesson. The
rhythmic pattern in this progression is two measures long rather than the
usual one measure. In other words, the rhythm of the first two measures is
repeated over and over. Notice that *root 4 bar chords* and *root 6 bar chords*
are used together. Watch the pick directions carefully.

Blues in A

One last new rhythm to learn. Start by playing four strums on each beat. Follow the pick directions and count.

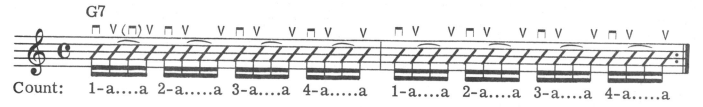

With this new rhythm the inside two wedge-marks are tied together. Keep counting the same way but leave out the "&": "1—a . . . a 2—a . . . a 3—a . . . a 4—a . . . a."

This is a difficult rhythm to play well so spend some time practicing the example. After you're sure you understand this new rhythm, start working on our very last standard rock progression. Take it through a few times on the slow side and play it finally at a moderate speed.

Blues in G

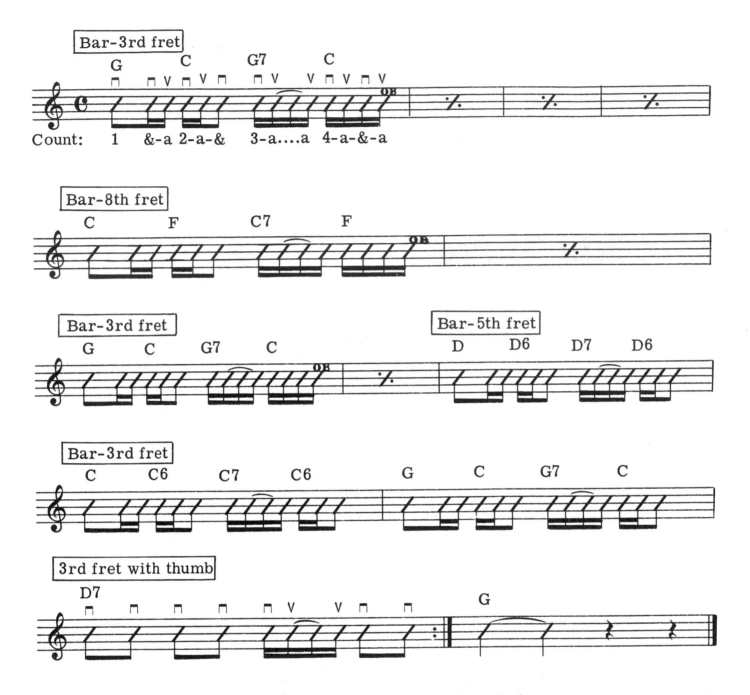

Syncopate the last beat in each measure for a slightly more interesting (and slightly more difficult) rhythm. This is quite a sophisticated rhythm.

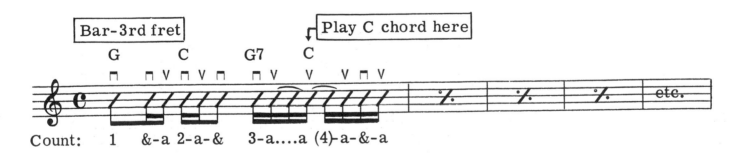

Play that last blues over using this syncopated rhythm.

The Slide Chord

One of the techniques frequently used by rhythm guitarists in today's rock sound is the slide chord. To understand the slide chord first play this example with the indicated rhythm.

Instead of actually strumming the A chord on the first beat, play the same chord one fret lower (4th fret instead of the 5th fret) on the last "&" of the previous measure and quickly slide the chord position up one fret without strumming the strings again. If the strings are allowed to keep vibrating, the left hand movement will change the pitch of the chord from Ab to A. This will be clearer to you as you play.

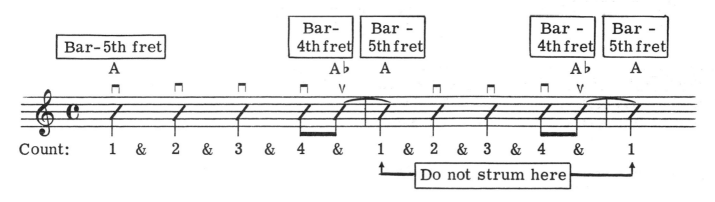

Remember that you don't strum on the "1" beat. To insure that the A chord will be heard, accent the Ab chord when you strum it. The tie mark between the Ab chord and the A chord indicates the slide chord.

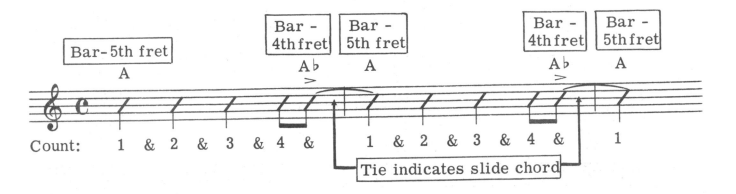

The slide chord is most effectively used with songs that are on the fast side. Work on this next blues to better understand when and where to play a slide chord. The rhythm is very similar to the one presented in the last lesson so it should present no new problems.

Blues in A

If using a slide chord one fret below the intended chord sounds nice to you, try the slide chord three frets below the intended chord. First play the A chord again counting as you play.

Starting on the "&" after the "3" beat, play an F# chord and slide up to the
G chord. On the "&" after the "4" beat, play an Ab chord and slide up to
the A chord on the first beat. Play this example very slowly making sure
that the first slide chord is completed before you play the second one. Try
this.

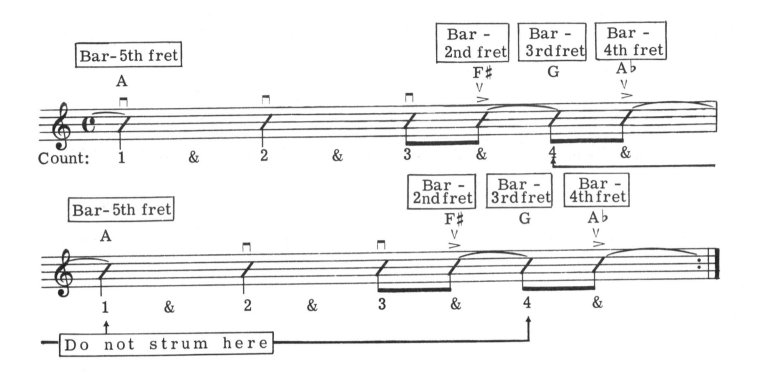

Now on to a very exciting progression that illustrates this new usage of the
slide chord. First play these two measures without using the slide chord.
Accent the A chord on the "&" after the "2" and play the second measure
with all staccato strums. As usual, watch the pick directions.

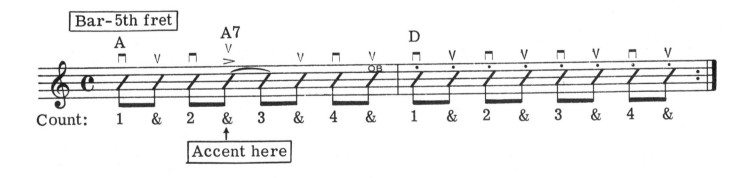

Make sure you can play the last example with ease before you attempt this
new progression. The total effect of this progression is quite exciting so
spend some time on it. Note the rhythmic interest the last two measures
add to the progression.

New Progression

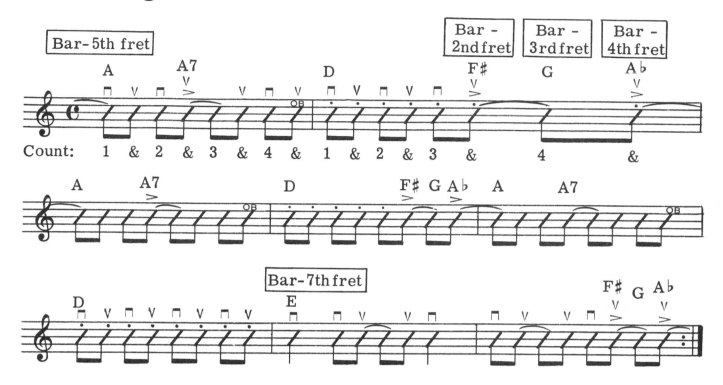

So instructive is the last chord progression let's take it again but starting with a *root 5 bar chord* this time. The same choice of slide chords, staccato strums, and accents are used. This is the last progression presented in this book so to convince yourself that you are a competent rhythm guitarist, see if you can play this progression fast and clean.

Last Progression

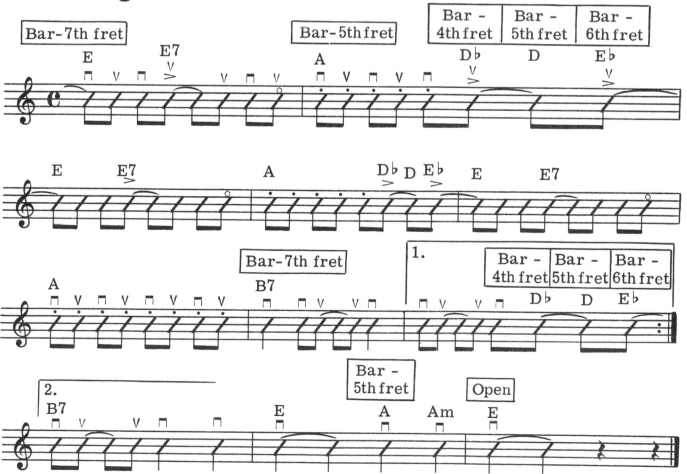

Finishing Touches

In this last lesson we'll examine some of the remaining techniques the professional rhythm guitarist uses. When you first start working on a song, try to keep the rhythm very simple. Try playing a down-stroke on the first beat of each measure to see if that's the type of feeling the song has.

Often playing a staccato strum on beats 2 and 4 is all a song needs.

Try accenting various beats to see if they add to the interest of the song. Accenting the "&" after the second beat is a favorite technique.

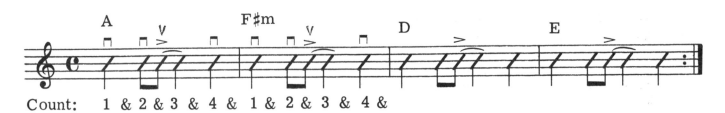

Count: 1 & 2 & 3 & 4 & 1 & 2 & 3 & 4 &

Accenting the "&" after the third beat is another popular technique. Remember at this stage to keep the rhythm simple.

Once you discover when to put in one accent, try adding a second one. Accenting the "2" and the "&" after the third beat is a popular rhythm.

Progression

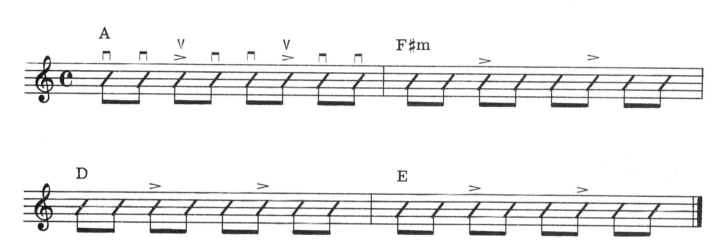

Of course, in order to figure out the best rhythm figure to play, you must listen very carefully to the singer. Once you have the basic rhythm you can dress it up with staccato strums, slide chords, percussive strums, and the various rhythms that we've covered in detail in this book. Remember, however, that often the simplest rhythm is the best. If you come up with a rhythm that you like very much for a particular song, it's a good idea to jot it down using the same rhythm symbols that we've been using. The next time you start working on that song, a glance at your notebook will give you the right rhythm guitar pattern.

One of the things you have to guard against when you play rock music is the tendency to speed-up once you've started a song. I've heard groups start a song off at a moderately fast speed and gradually, over the course of the song, increase the speed until they were playing so fast they could hardly keep up with themselves. This comes from not listening to each other. You overcome this tendency by trying to play the song slower as you go along.

Another thing that you should be able to do is change the key of a song. Very frequently the singer will request that you play the song in a higher (or lower) key. Examine this next chart.

Chord Chart

CHORD NUMBER					
I	IV	V	VI	II	III
C (C Maj 7)	F (F Maj 7)	G (G7)	Am (Am7)	Dm (Dm7)	Em (Em7)
D (D Maj 7)	G (G Maj 7)	A (A7)	Bm (Bm7)	Em (Em7)	F# (F#m7)
E (E Maj 7)	A (A Maj 7)	B (B7)	C#m (C#m7)	F#m (F#m7)	G#m (G#m7)
F (F Maj 7)	Bb (Bb Maj 7)	C (C7)	Dm (Dm7)	Gm (Gm7)	Am (Am7)
G (G Maj 7)	C (C Maj 7)	D (D7)	Em (Em7)	Am (Am7)	Bm (Bm7)
A (A Maj 7)	D (D Maj 7)	E (E7)	F#m (F#m7)	Bm (Bm7)	C#m (C#m7)
Bb (Bb Maj 7)	Eb (Eb Maj 7)	F (F7)	Gm (Gm7)	Cm (Cm7)	Dm (Dm7)

(Row labels at left: Key of C, Key of D, Key of E, Key of F, Key of G, Key of A, Key of Bb)

This chart lists all the chords in the most popular rock keys. The chords in parentheses are the 7th chord substitutions. When you want to change the key of a song the first thing you must determine is the original key of the song. With the blues and turn around progressions, the first chord in the song tells you the key. Most other progressions follow the same formula. Examine this chord progression:

Progression *

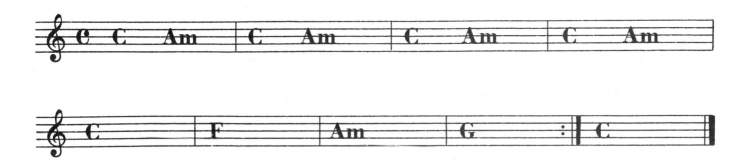

*This type of chord chart omits the rhythm guitar indications. It can be used by the bass, organ, lead, or rhythm guitar player. Because there are two chords in the first measure, it is understood that each chord is held for two beats.

Both the first and the last chord in the progression are C chords so the progression is in the key of C. See if you can locate the chords in the progression on our chart. On the line belonging to the Key of C, the C chord is the I chord, the Am chord is the VI chord, the F chord is the IV chord, and the G chord is the V chord. To change the pitch of the progression, use the corresponding chords in the new key. To raise the progression to the key of E use the I chord (E chord), the VI chord (C#m chord), the IV chord (A chord), and the V chord (B chord).

Another popular method of changing keys is to learn the progression in the original key using all bar chords. To raise the progression up two frets, simply play all the bar chords up two frets. To lower the progression, follow the same procedure in reverse.

Appendix A (Discography)

Here's a list of rock groups and records that you should be familiar with. These records provide an excellent foundation for any rock musician's record library. These are the best records of every style on the rock scene today. These LP's are the best of the best. Like everything involved in pop culture, styles change and new groups come on the scene so you'll have to augment this selection from time to time. Pick out and buy one or more records from each category and, more important, listen to them, listen to them, listen to them.

Modern American

Jimi Hendrix, *Jimi Hendrix Experience Smash Hits* (Reprise 2025)
Country Joe & the Fish, *Electric Music for the Mind and Body* (Vanguard 79244)
The Doors, *The Doors* (Elektra 74007)
Big Brother and the Holding Company, *Cheap Thrills* (Columbia 9700)
The Allman Brothers, *Idlewild South* (Atco 33-342)
John McLaughlin, *The Inner Mounting Flame* (Columbia 31067)
Santana, *Abraxas* (Columbia 30130)

The Detroit Soul Sound

The Mar-keys & Booker T. & the MG's, *Back to Back* (Stax 720)
Otis Redding, *Dictionary of Soul* (Volt 415)
Wilson Pickett, *The Best of Wilson Pickett* (Atlantic 8151)
Sam & Dave, *The Best of Sam & Dave* (Atlantic 8218)
Blood, Sweat & Tears, *Greatest Hits* (Columbia 31170)
James Brown, *Greatest Hits* (King 8452)
Sly & the Family Stone, *Greatest Hits* (Epic 30325)

Folk Rock

Jefferson Airplane, *Surrealistic Pillow* (RCA 3766)
Crosby, Stills & Nash, *Crosby, Stills & Nash* (Atlantic 8229)
Grateful Dead, *Workingman's Dead* (Warner Bros. 1869)
Bob Dylan, *Bob Dylan's Greatist Hits* (Columbia 9463 & 31120)
Donovan, *Greatest Hits* (Epic 26439)

Blues Bands

B. B. King, *Live at the Regal* (ABC-Paramount 509)
Blues Breakers, *Blues Breakers* (London 492)
Charley Musselwhite's Southside Band, *Stand Back!* (Vanguard 79232)
The Paul Butterfield Blues Band, *What's Shakin'* (Elektra 4002)
T. Bone Walker, *The Truth* (Brunswick 754126)
Johnny Winter, *Johnny Winter And* (Columbia 30221)
Taj Mahal, *The Natch'l Blues* (Columbia 9698)
Albert King, *Live Wire / Blues Power* (Stax 2003)

Traditional Rhythm 'n Blues

History of Rhythm & Blues (Atlantic 8161, 8162, 8163, 8164)
Chicago / The Blues / Today! (Vanguard 9216)
The Blues (Cadet 4026, 4027, 4034)
Elmo James, *The Sky is Crying* (Sphere 7002)
Slim Harpo, *Raining in My Heart* (Excello 8003)
Jimmy Reed, *The Best of Jimmy Reed* (Vee Jay SR 1039)
Chuck Berry, *Chuck Berry's Greatest Hits* (Chess 1485)
Jr. Walker & the All Stars, *Greatest Hits* (Soul 718)

Modern English

The Beatles, *Sgt. Pepper's Lonely Hearts Club Band* (Capitol 2653)
The Rolling Stones, *Big Hits* (London NP-1)
Ten Years After, *Ssssh. Ten Years After* (London 18029)
The Who, *Tommy* (Decca 7205)
Alice Cooper, *Killer* (Warner Bros. 2567)
Jeff Beck, *Jeff Beck Group* (Epic 31331)
Eric Clapton, *History* (Atco 803)
Emerson, Lake & Palmer, *Tarkus* (Cotillion 9900)
Jethro Tull, *Benefit* (Reprise 6400)
Moody Blues, *Every Good Boy Deserves Favor* (Threshold 5)

Appendix B Suggestions for Buying a Guitar

Suggestions for buying a guitar . . . .

There are two types of rock 'n roll guitars: the solid body and the semi-hollow body.

The solid body guitar has a very "funky" sound, and is preferred by blues bands and hard-rock groups. It produces very intense high notes, and the metallic, wailing quality makes it an excellent lead guitar as well as a hard and gutty rhtyhm guitar.

The semi-hollow body has some of the qualities of an acoustic guitar, and has a softer, mellower tone. This characteristic makes it a better instrument for the jazz or folk influenced rock styles prevalent among many of today's bands. It should be remembered that it is the guitarist that controls the sound, and, with some experimentation with your gutiar and amplifier, you should be able to get any sound you want out of your instrument.

Some professionals like to use a regular round-hole acoustic guitar with a built-in pick-up for certain sounds and effects. The quality of the tone here is very close to that of the unamplified guitar but, of course, much louder. Many country-western and "rock-a-billy" groups have pick-ups installed in their Martins and Gibsons, and bridge the gap between country and rock music. This is also used by several prominent folk rock artists where the sound is consistent with the music and their particular style. It is, however, very limiting for the all-around rock 'n roll guitarist.

Before you decide which to buy, try out several different makes and types of guitars at a music store. The kind of guitar you get will greatly affect the sound of your music, so the decision is an important one.

Once you have decided on the type of guitar you want, there is still the problem of getting the best guitar for your money. If you have never bought a guitar before, I would strongly urge you to take a guitar-playing friend or teacher to the store with you. Here are several important things to look for before buying a guitar:

Is the neck perfectly straight? Sight along the fingerboard from the nut as if you were aiming a rifle. You will be able to see if the neck is bent or twisted in any way. A warped neck will usually mean that the frets are not in correct tune, which will be a problem later one. For good luck, turn the guitar around and check it again from the bridge to the nut.

Most of the better guitars have an adjustable rod built into the neck to prevent warping.

Are the frets in tune? Pluck each string open, and then fretted at the 12th fret. The notes should be perfect octaves. If the two notes don't sound in tune, the frets might not be placed properly, or the neck might be warped. If the guitar has a movable bridge, it might only need readjusting. But these are questions for a person experienced in these matters.

Is the action too high or too low? Many electric guitars have devices that allow you to adjust the action (distance of the strings from the fingerboard). If the action is too high, it will be difficult to fret the strings properly, especially with bar chords. If it is too low, your strings will buzz (hit the frets while vibrating) and the tone will be poor. If the action is not comfortable one way or the other, see if the bridge can be adjusted to make the strings higher or lower. On some guitars there will be a screw at the place where the neck joins the body, which changes the angle of the neck, thereby changing the action. If these features are not built into the guitar and the action is not right, a qualified repair man would be needed to change it. It would probably be better to buy a different guitar.

Other things to check: Are the frets smooth and of even height? Do the volume and tone controls work easily and noiselessly? How about the tuning pegs—are they easy to turn, and do they tune the strings evenly and accurately?

These things are all important; much more important than the size, shape, color, and designs and fancy decorations that adorn some electric guitars.

Amplifiers

If you're a rock musician you'll need an amplifier. There are many inexpensive amps you can get to practice with, and if you're really strung out for cash, you can even play your guitar through a radio or T.V. (The sound's not fantastic, but at least you can hear yourself play.) When you are ready to join a group, you'll have to buy a better amp. It's important that you have one that does not distort or blow out at high volumes and that has reverb. If you can afford one that has vibrato and super-treble, so much the better.

Do yourself a favor: when you are ready to play in a group, buy yourself the best equipment you can afford. Cheap guitars and amps will cost you more money in the long run than you saved by buying them. I recommend Fender for solid body guitars, Gibson or Guild for semi-hollow body guitars. If you are buying an acoustic, Martins and Gibsons are my choice.

The best amps are made by Fender, Sunn, and Traynor.

Appendix C (Chord Diagrams)

Here is a complete catalogue of all the important chords used
in rock 'n roll. In the first section are the open chords (chords
using open strings), and in the second section are the bar chords.

Open Chords

Em	Em6	Em7	E	E6	E7	E9	G	G7	Am

 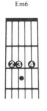   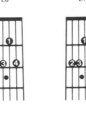   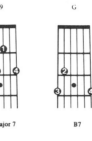 

Am6	Am7	A	A6	A7	A7	A Major 7	B7	C	C7

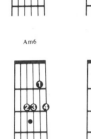 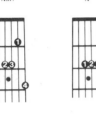   

Dm	D	D7	F

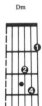   

Moveable Chords

ROOT 6 CHORDS

Major chord (F)	6th chord (F6)	7th chord (F7)	9th chord (F9)	minor chord (Fm)	minor 6th chord (Fm6)	minor 7th chord (Fm7)	Major 7th chord (G Major 7)

ROOT 5 CHORDS

Major chord (Bb)	6th chord (Bb6)	7th chord (Bb7)	Major 7th chord (Bb Major 7)	minor chord (Bbm)	minor 6th chord (Bbm6)	minor 7th chord (Bbm7)	9th chord (B9)	7th chord (C7)

ROOT 4 CHORDS

minor chord (Ebm)	7th chord (Eb7)	diminished chord (Eb dim)	augmented chord (F aug)

2/88